Growl of the Tiger

ARDENNES – ALSACE **RHINELAND** **CENTRAL EUROPE**

Tenth Armored Division's Epic Stories of Combat

in World War II in Europe,

as recalled by

Major (Retired) Dean M. Chapman

1993

Foreword

This book was almost never written! For years I could neither write about nor discuss my experiences in World War II. It was not uncommon for me, in the middle of the night, to wake suddenly from a sound sleep and find myself sitting bolt upright in bed bathed in cold sweat, re-living again those screams of burned and wounded men and officers of some battle long, long ago. At such times I had to rise and walk the floor until my nerves settled down once again. Gradually, time healed both my fears and tears.

By the time our two sons were in high school, I began to tell some of these stories. Every member of my family urged me to write about them. Encouragement also came from several war-time friends. These included Owen McBride, who was the Captain of "B" Battery of the Four Hundred Twenty Third Armored Field Artillery Battalion of our Tenth Armored Division. He was the first officer I reported to as a very green second lieutenant. Over the intervening years, Owen and I have become the best of friends. Another friend from the Division Headquarters who encouraged me was Lieutenant Colonel William Eckles, who was our (G-2) Intelligence Officer.

For my readers to use this book with ease, it is divided into two sections. The first entitled "From New York Harbor to the Zugspitze", contains stories of battles in chronological sequence. These stories and reminiscences are not meant to be technical logs, but rather interesting recollections of events, men and officers who played pivotal roles in many successful battles of that great war. As the only aide to the Commanding General of our great Tenth Armored Division, during all of the fighting from Metz onward, I was privy to much information never before revealed.

The second section of this book — Reflections Ponderings, and Musings — consists of random stories about many men and officers. Some stories are humorous, some sad and some speak of our great love of country and compassion for each other.

A book of this nature would not be complete without a tribute to the First Lady of our Tenth Armored Division, Mrs. Priscilla Newgarden, the widow of General Paul Newgarden. She still comes to our annual reunions and is dearly loved by all. In the spring of 1991 she broke her arm playing tennis. By our Division's Labor Day reunion that year, she not only arrived on time for the festivities, but also informed us she had already begun playing tennis again. For a "young lady" approaching her ninetieth birthday, she is a most remarkable person.

The poem "America, Beloved Land" was written by my mother-in-law, Mrs. L.O. Poole. Besides being an excellent poet, she was also a fine artist. This poem, like most of hers, was published in the Sunday Edition of the "Omaha World Herald" newspaper, during the years 1930 through 1948. At age eighty, she collected all her poems and published them in "Bits of Life" circa 1974.

This book is dedicated to all the fine men and officers who were the great Tenth Armored Division. I would like to single out two persons for special mention here — Wally Bunt and Billy E. Hanel. Along with myself, they graduated in 1943 from

Michigan State University. The three of us were assigned to the Tenth Armored Division and so we fought the war across Europe together.

I sincerely hope you will enjoy my descriptions of events, character studies, observations and commentaries, insights, and just my stories and ruminations! Here goes, —

A special thank you must be given to my friends, Theodore Ridley and Wilma Kyvig for proof-reading this book. Also, I give credit to my dear wife, Shirley, who labored many hours to type and re-type it.

AMERICA, BELOVED LAND

America, America, beloved land
Whose birth made suffering people free
Born from rebelling pain and strife
To glory reaching out from sea to sea.

America, the hour once more has come
The time to justify thy holy birth
To prove the cause for which our father died
Is great enough to cover all the earth.

America, so noble, great and fine
Fight on against the enemies without, within
Nor let a despot's cruelty and power
Deter us from the good, since we must win.

Fight on until you wear the victor's crown
Fight on till all the men of earth are free
Remembering your heritage of right
And grateful to the God of liberty.

by Laurel O. Poole
1974

The Author
Dean M. Chapman

Dean M. Chapman was born in Lansing, Michigan on June 20, 1920. He graduated from Michigan State University in June of 1943, where he completed the senior R.O.T.C. course. With the war engulfing this country, no cadets were to receive commissions as second lieutenants directly upon graduation because summer field training had been eliminated between junior and senior years. On March 1, 1943 all the senior R.O.T.C. cadets at Michigan State University were taken to Fort Wayne in Detroit,

Dean M. Chapman – Then...

given physicals, and sworn in as privates. They then returned to college and billeted as privates with all chores except K.P. After graduation, they were sent to basic infantry training until there was room as the appropriate O.C.S. Dean graduated from Fort Sill, Oklahoma with class 90 on December 10, 1943. Shortly thereafter,

...and Now

he volunteered for the Tenth Armored Division at Camp Gordon, Georgia. There he was assigned to "B" Battery of the Four Hundred Twenty Third Armored Field Artillery Battalion and later became the Aide to General Morris, our Commanding General, and continued as such all during combat.

At present he lives with his wife, Shirley, in Muskegon, Michigan.

ISBN: 978-1-68162-124-1
Library of Congress
Catalog Card Number: 94-60920

TABLE OF CONTENTS

Foreword
America, Beloved Land

Section 1
FROM NEW YORK HARBOR TO THE ZUGSPITZE

TABLE OF CONTENTS

Section 2
REFLECTIONS, PONDERINGS AND MUSINGS

TABLE OF CONTENTS

Section 1

FROM NEW YORK HARBOR

TO THE ZUGSPITZE

1
Ferry Boat Whistle Stop

All day long officers and men of our Tenth Armored Division slowly climbed single file up the six story high Navy Pier stairs to reach the "Alexander's" gangplank, then crossed over on that ramp to walk down five or six stories to their assigned spot inside the ship. All this time each was carrying his duffle bag on his shoulders. When we began our climb up those bags weighed about sixty pounds but later in the day I swear they weighed one hundred pounds.

The stairs on this pier were all open to the weather. It was a gray day and spitting rain off and on. It took the better part of daylight that day to load this old "Alexander". It had been a German ship that the British had seized as a prize of war in 1914. The engines were the steam reciprocating type. About dark, on 11 September, 1944, the ship began to move away from the pier in preparation for high tide which was due later that evening. The ship was a large roomy vessel. Our contingent fitted in quite well even though all of us were bunked five high having barely two feet between our bunk and the next one above. Officers and men were in different sections of the ship but everyone had identical bunk set-ups.

As soon as the ship began to move the loud speaker issued the following orders: All port holes must be closed, locked, and black-out curtains put up from sundown until daylight. A "shift" was set up for a few men to go top side during daylight hours.

Time on deck would be no longer than thirty minutes. Each man and officer would be allotted one pint of fresh water per day. We could drink it, wash our socks in it, or shave. Salt water showers would be available after we were at sea. Each section's number would be called twice a day for the two meals. All officers and men would be fed separately during these staggered shifts. We had to take our mess kits. Our first meal was to be breakfast the next day.

After setting in and putting up the black-out curtains, there was not much to do except write letters and play cards. Even for such limited activity, we were cramped for space. With so many troops on board, we could not even stroll about the ship. At this point most of us turned in with the rhythmical throb of the ship's big engines lulling us to dreamland.

Sometime before daylight, I awoke and realized those engines were silent. Occasionally I could hear someone on deck shouting. As it grew lighter, we opened the port holes and to our amazement we were looking at the Statue of Liberty nearby. I was told that a British liner had entered the harbor too far over on our side of the channel and in order to avoid a collision, our ship's captain had edged a little too far and we had run aground.

A typical scenario was then played out. Tug boats attached lines trying to free us. Our ship, with open full throttle in reverse and the tugs pulling, would not budge because she was too heavily loaded. It was then we received the order to "abandon ship". We climbed up those five or six stories onto the deck where we clambered over the side, duffle and all, via landing nets, onto New York Harbor Ferries.

Once on those ferries, we thought we had it made. Not so!

Once on those ferries, we thought we had it made. Not so!
These ferries took us to the middle of New York Harbor where
we all had to climb again onto different ferry boats as a different
union controlled that half of the harbor. This move made our
blood boil as all of us were on our way to fight and perhaps die
for freedom's cause. The least the labor unions could have done
would be to ease our burden a bit. Additionally, it would have
been good "public relations" for them to accommodate us.

You guessed it! The second group of ferries took us right
back to the same pier from which we had just loaded yesterday.
So we had the same "climb up" duffle bag and all. This time we
were all crowded into a newer, faster, smaller vessel. We loaded
into the S.S. Brazil. This ship had been built in the 1920's to
accommodate the tourist trade from New York to Rio de Janeiro
and return. This ship was a narrow speedster and could do
twenty knots instead of ten as was true of the old Alexander.

By this delay, we had missed our convoy to Europe. They
had journeyed on without us. Our ship's captain ran at full
throttle to try and catch the convoy. We zig-zagged across the
Atlantic with only one small Navy destroyer escort leading the
way.

The first day out of New York almost witnessed a mutiny
— not by the ship's crew, but by our enlisted men. The first meal
served them was terrible. One of the items was applesauce. The
ship's galley had cooked the apples with skins, cores, stems, and
worms all together. One of our non-commissioned officers was
so incensed he took his mess kit with this uneaten meal to his
battalion commander to show him what it looked like. Our
Division had always insisted upon good chow for our troops.

This fired up the Lieutenant Colonel and he took this sergeant and his mess gear to the Division Commanding General who had a conference with that ship's captain.

The next day the food was better, applesauce, yes, but no skins, cores, stems, nor worms.

My guess was they cooked the apples as before, then strained out the debris. No one became ill so perhaps it was okay the second time around.

More insidious was my next idea. Could it have been possible that all savings over a specified amount became a basis of a bonus for the ship's captain? No one will probably know. With the great numbers of G.I.'s going over, such a possibility could have been real.

About the third day out, our Navy lads sighted what they thought was an enemy periscope off our starboard (right) bow. At this the escort as well as the two Navy gun crews located topside of the Brazil began firing at it. Actually, it turned out to be only a floating wooden box - not an enemy submarine. All were much relieved to observe our Navy men blow this box out of the sea. Their accuracy was reassuring. The rest of our trip was uneventful.

We did actually join up with our convoy just outside Land's End, England. I shall never forget that sight. There were hundreds of ships in a hollow square as far as eye could see. Destroyer and Navy escorts were weaving in and out checking for enemy subs. At Land's End our ship slowed to take on an English pilot who was to guide us through the Allied mine fields to Cherbourg, France. This taking on consisted of our ships dropping a line over the side. The upper end of the line was fastened to an arm which was pivoted out over the water. The pilot grabbed this line and climbed up to the arm where pilot and arm were both swung aboard. As this pilot appeared to be in his mid fifty's and his climb up was a good hundred and twenty feet, we all cheered him aboard.

Our next stop was the roadstead off Cherbourg, France. This end of the line was a lot different from New York Harbor. Cherbourg was badly damaged. No ships the size of our could enter its harbor. The wharf was in ruins due to Navy gun fire and Air Corp bombs. Floating mines were everywhere and our mine sweepers were busy every day clearing this harbor so that our troops could be brought ashore safely. The Germans had not only left the usual floating mines in that harbor, but also had mines that were anchored on the bottom. Every few hours these anchored mines were ratcheted upward a few feet. These mines were usually a non-magnetic type and so were hard to locate. Our Navy began its daily mine sweeping operation in mid June, 1944, and carried it on until the end of June, 1945. After twelve months of daily sweeping the channel and Port of Cherbourg, France, these water areas were finally declared free of all naval mines. Barges pushed by tugs and/or Army ducks carried us in. Once ashore, we were marched inland about two miles where we set up camp.

We went ashore in the middle of the night (about 2 a.m.) and we marched inland in a pouring rain to a Red Cross reception area for coffee and doughnuts. These were served in the rain without benefit of shelter. Only after that were we ordered to proceed to our camp area. Lt. Wally Bunt set up his tent in the dark as did everyone else. In the morning light he discovered he had strategically located his tent between two "cow pies".

This was the hedge row area of France.

2
Terrify and Destroy

Our Tenth Armored Division of the Army was really an "elite unit" from top to bottom. There were several reasons for this "label". First and foremost were the superior type of men and officers composing it. Not only were they well above average intelligence for a Division of our size, but every man and officer was extremely well trained to do the kind of warfare required.

Historically, Major General Paul W. Newgarden activated and assumed command of our Tenth Armored Division on 15 July, 1942 at Ft. Benning, Georgia. He was a polished and outstanding leader. He demanded and received perfection of war skills through tough training, while exuding personal charisma which could put one at ease or "peel the hide off one's back side". While doing either, one had the feeling that he was like a benevolent father doing it for our own good. Additionally, he was one of the younger major generals being only in his early fifties. At West Point, he earned a black belt in amateur boxing.

One of the reasons his men and officers respected him is revealed by this example: After our Division had moved to Camp Gordon, Georgia, on 5 September, 1943 for final training, it rained hard one weekend. The General and his wife, Priscilla, were returning to Camp Gordon from nearby Augusta, where they had attended church services. Passing the bus stop in Augusta, he saw one of his very wet soldiers waiting for the bus to return to camp. General Newgarden immediately stopped his car and invited this private to ride along. Not only did he take this man back to camp, he delivered him directly to his barracks. This was as unprecedented for most Generals as it was typical for General Newgarden. One can only imagine the feelings of that young private and his peers.

Priscilla Newgarden was a "lady" in her own right, also. One story from 1944 days at Camp Gordon comes to mind. A certain young captain's wife was obviously pregnant. It was a hot day and all wives were invited to attend a parade. The young captain's wife had little understanding of military duties of officers' wives. She had been married only about a year and most of that time she had stayed at home, only recently coming to the camp.

This young wife was hot and uncomfortable. She saw a chair in the shade in the reviewing area, so she sat down. Shortly thereafter, along came Priscilla. The chair was meant for her but she immediately sized up the situation and refused to let the adjutant remove the young wife. Mrs. Newgarden graciously sat in the hot sun with the other wives. This act was not lost on either wives or men of our Division.

In January, 1944, I, as a lieutenant, was attached for training to the "B" Battery of the Four Hundred Twenty Third Armored Field Artillery Battalion of this Tenth Armored Division. Many other lieutenants of all branches were "attached for training" to the Division. Somewhat prior to this, about 2000 enlisted men were also attached for training. These enlisted men all had I.Q.'s of about 120 and had been students for several months at various American universities as "guests of Uncle Sam" where they were taught trigonometry, English, map reading and other related subjects. The purpose of this program was to train them for future use in the Army and to hold them in a state of readiness. They all had basic training prior to their college training.

Once attached to our Division, all of us (officers and enlisted men) were engaged in our regular Armored Division training program, then we were sent to our various battalions, i.e. infantry, tanks, artillery, engineers, etc., within our Division where these practical skills were again honed. These skills were "march, maneuver and shoot".

On 14 July, 1944, General Newgarden and Colonel Laurence were tragically killed in a crash of their light plane returning to Camp Gordon from Washington, D.C. The General had with him the orders for our Division to stage in New York City for combat in Europe five weeks later.

About three weeks later, Major General Wm. H.H. Morris, Jr., assumed the command of our Division. I never knew who was responsible, but soon after General Morris took over, there was a general review and re-assignment of officers and enlisted men within our Division. All of those 2000 men who had previously been "attached for training", plus most of the junior officers who likewise had been "attached for training" were given assignments in our Division. At the same time, all the unqualified enlisted men and officers were transferred. This action did not affect the command structure, as all of our top officers were excellent leaders and thus were retained.

The result of this change of personnel was to raise the average I.Q. of all enlisted men. One has merely to review the Army policy of how a new division is created to appreciate fully this change. A new division is started by assembling a cadre or corp of key people. Then the "fillers" are assigned. In most cases, these fillers are largely composed of men having lower I.Q.'s and lower educational levels. This practice occurred originally with our Division, but this newly assigned group of men and better trained junior officers made us into an "elite unit" by anyone's definition.

I always believed the aforementioned change was the behind-the-scene work of our new Major General Morris. He was a considerably older man than Newgarden, since at the time of his taking charge of our Division he was nearly sixty years old. He had graduated with the class of 1911 from West Point, served in World War I as an infantry officer at the front. Now he was to fight on the same ground against the same enemy in World War II. Sometime between these wars, he transferred from infantry to armor. He commanded and trained an armored regiment, an armored division, and a corp in preparation to beat General Rommel in North Africa. Just before staging to sail to North Africa, Rommel's army was defeated and so his armored corp was no longer needed. General Morris, seeing the turn of events, volunteered to step down from being a corp commander in this country by asking the Army Chief-of-Staff for command of the first available armored division that was to go overseas. This turned out to be our Tenth Armored Division, due to General Newgarden's untimely death.

It was obvious to any casual observer that General Morris operated differently from our original Commanding General because he was much older and had his World War I experience. He had been a War Department observer at

Salerno, Italy. Much earlier as a R.O.T.C. instructor at Texas A. & M., General Morris was credited with introducing basketball as a sport at that university where he became known as the "father of basketball". He was an accomplished ballroom dancer and all the ladies enjoyed having him for their partner as he was also tall and graceful - no doubt his basketball expertise added to his social gracefulness! General Morris was tall (six feet and one inch) and slim. Our original Commanding General was somewhat shorter and stockier. Both generals were always "gentlemen".

Most of our troops never became acquainted with General Morris as we sailed for Europe about five weeks after he took command. We were fortunate in having an experienced general of his stature. His staff work and general knowledge of the enemy was excellent. He spoke French fluently and had good relations with the French army and people. He had been awarded the Croix-de-guerre medal in World War I for his battlefield leadership. Like General Newgarden, he had intuitive sense to select and retain excellent top officers to work for him.

To justify our motto "Terrify and Destroy", it will help to understand its full impact if I describe the Division's accomplishments citing its abilities.

The third and last commander of our Division was Major General Prickett. When General Morris was promoted to Commanding General of VI Corp at the conclusion of combat duty in Europe, General Prickett was assigned to replace him. His job was to close out and dissolve our Division, destroy all its records, and ship men home. Our elite Division was disbanded "over there", which was most unfortunate.

At the conclusion of war in Europe on V E Day, I overheard General Morris tell a visiting officer friend that our Tenth Armored Division succeeded in taking all of the Division Combat objectives either on time or ahead of schedule. We held the record for all Divisions on the western front of having the largest combat loss per day. To the uninitiated reader, this record may appear to be due to poor leadership. In reality, this is not true when all the facts are considered. Taking our objectives on schedule indicates that we did our job correctly. The large loss per day reveals that we had a tough battle winning each and every one. Had there been fewer or no losses, it would have indicated that we faced little or no opposition.

The losses and fast taking of our objectives, however, tells the whole story; anyone having completed Command & Staff School will recognize this fact.

The question has been asked, "If the Tenth Armored Division was so competent, how does it happen that no one ever heard of it?" The answer is revealed in one of those unusual quirks of war. After the first series of battles in which our Division engaged and which concluded in the capture of Metz, France, General Eisenhower placed us on status known as "S.H.A.E.F. Secret Reserve". This meant that we removed all Division shoulder patches and painted out our Division markings on vehicles. No reference could be made of us by any news source. Thus, we were literally "blacked-out". At this time, General Eisenhower also "loaned" us to General Patton's Third Army for its use. Patton could use us any way he chose with one stipulation; should Ike wish us returned to him to be used elsewhere as S.H.A.E.F. reserve, Patton had only 24 hours to do so.

Patton's answer to this stipulation was strictly "Pattonesque". Patton immediately decided that the only way he could keep us was to put our Division in the vanguard of his Third Army and keep us continually in combat. By so doing, he reasoned that it would be both impossible and impracticable to release us within the 24 hour time frame. This situation, of course, contributed to many battle casualties.

It must be pointed out that General Patton used our Division as his point or lead unit. When our Division was later attached to General Patch's Seventh U.S. Army, we were still the point.

Because of our Division's great ability to move and strike swiftly in another sector 75 - 100 miles away in all kinds of weather, the German Command began to refer to our Tenth Armored Division as "The Ghost Division". An excellent example of this label was our night withdrawal from the Saar-Mossel Triangle battlefield and moving 75 miles in total blackout and radio silence over crowning black top and ice covered roads through snow storms and fog to eastern Luxembourg. Here we attacked elements of the Fifth Panzer Army. This attack through the Fourth U.S. Infantry Division occurred before daylight the following morning, resulting in a classic operation by any standard.

3
Sparks of Genius - - Fires of Hell!

To the uninitiated in modern warfare, the dagger-like attack of an American armored division is an awesome operation; this was especially true of our Tenth Armored Division. We called ourselves "The Tiger Division" and our motto was "Terrify and Destroy". This we did to the hated Nazis on a regular basis all across Europe.

We were a "triangular" division; which meant structurally (Tables of Organization) that we had three infantry battalions, three tank battalions, three armored artillery battalions plus others, i.e. a company of signal men, a battalion of engineers, and a reconnaissance squadron, a M.P. company trained for combat and one or more medium artillery battalions were attached. Attached on a permanent basis was a battalion of anti-aircraft, a battalion of tank destroyers, an air controller from the air corp who coordinated its attack fighters and bombers with our movements, an enemy interrogation team and an order of battle team. Medical evacuation units were added, as were other special units such as truck companies as situations required.

All of the above were headed up by our Division Headquarters. From them, lines of authority flowed down to three combat commands known as CC-A, CC-B, and CC-R. Below these C.C.s were three infantry and three tank, and three artillery battalions, and others. In combat, our Division

Headquarters was actually re-constituted as follows:

Forward Division Headquarters consisted of the Commanding General and G-1, G-2, G-3, and G-4, and chief of staff. The complete G-2 (intelligence of the enemy) and G-3 staff sections (plans and training) were always at the forward division's headquarters.

Division Rear contained all the detail G-1 (personnel clerks) personnel, G-4 (supply personnel), G-5 section (military government), Division Trains, Division Band, and numerous supply, maintenance, and truck companies.

Division Artillery Headquarters was what the name implied and usually controlled all the artillery battalions and their firing of concentrations. Division Artillery Headquarters was often found between the Forward Division Headquarters and Rear Division Headquarters and adjacent to the three artillery firing battalions.

One of the first things General Morris did, as our Division Commander, was to change our infantry and tank battalions from a basis of table of organization to specialized "Task Forces". This was accomplished by taking an infantry battalion headquarters and headquarters company with three infantry companies, deleting the remainder of the infantry companies of that battalion and adding three tank companies. This reorganization meant that one Lieutenant Colonel Battalion Commander of infantry had under his direct "line" control both infantry and tanks. The same change was made with the tank battalion which now consisted of a tank battalion headquarters and headquarters company with three tank companies plus the three infantry companies taken from the infantry battalion above. Thus, a lieutenant colonel battalion commander of tanks now commanded both tanks and infantry. To distinguish between these new Task Forces, the lieutenant colonels' name was used, i.e. Task Force Chamberlain and Task Force Richardson, etc.

Within each Task Force (battalion size) were several companies, each under a captain of infantry or tanks. The same breakdown followed here as in the larger battalion sized Task Force. One would have an infantry headquarters and headquarters platoon, plus three rifle platoons plus three platoons of tanks. This unit was then under a Task Force and referred to as a "Team". The name of its commanding officer was used as a designation, i.e. Team Hyduke, etc.

The above alterations may seem complicated to the non-military minded, but they had very real significance in combat. A line officer was now in direct command of both infantry and tanks at the battalion level thus preventing the old "Alphonso-Gaston" syndrome. Previous to the creation of a Task Force confusion was a common occurrence when the order was given "to attack", i.e. the infantry battalion would wait for the tanks to move forward and the tank battalion would hold back for the infantry battalion to move. Under the Task Force system (as above) when the order was issued "to attack", no unit hesitated as both infantry and tanks were under the same line officer at the battalion level. These Task Forces moved out as a united force, functioning like a hand in a glove. This unity was necessary for success as now the infantry protected the tanks from enemy anti-tank grenades and the tanks protected the infantry from 88 mm. assault guns and machine-gun fire.

Our enlisted men and officers exhibited "can do" enthusiasm on the battle field which resulted in delivering to the Nazi soldiers the "fire of hell".

By way of explaining the amount of effort that had to be exerted on an average day of combat, our Tenth Armored Division expended 700 tons of shot and shell. This required 288 two and a half ton truck loads. In addition, our heavy tanks each had fuel tanks that held 250 gallons of high test aviation gasoline. Every day we used 25,000 gallons of this fuel and it had to be delivered in five gallon cans, plus 15,000 gallons of regular gasoline for trucks, jeeps, armored cars, and infantry half-tracks also delivered daily in five gallon cans. To all of this must be added one box of "C" rations for each squad and/or vehicle, plus one five gallon can of potable water, plus one "K" ration (emergency ration) which included fourteen sheets of toilet paper to each man and officer, plus medical supplies, signal supplies, and maintenance supplies, i.e. barrels of grease and oil for tank and truck transmissions and gear boxes.

I often wondered how they determined that each man and officer required 14 sheets of toilet paper daily. I have often thought I would like to see their experiments —— on second thought I guess I would just as soon not be privy to this research. The quantity did however appear to be sufficient!

Some results of this "Fire of Hell" delivery were:

Captured 56,000 Nazi soldiers as prisoners.
Captured 650 towns and cities.
Captured the first major German city - Tier
on March 2, 1945.
Participated in the capture of Metz. The first

time the Metz fortress had been captured in 1500 years.

Played the major role in the epic defense of Bastogne. (The One Hundred First Airborne received all the credit as our Division was on Secret S.H.A.E.F. reserve and no details were allowed to be published.) Nevertheless, without our heavy tanks and guns the One Hundred First Division could never have held Bastogne. We were the first Division sent north by General Patton to halt and stop the 5th Panzer Army's attack on Bastogne.

The price of peace to our Division was:

> 642 killed in action
>
> 132 died from wounds
>
> 10 died during capture
>
> 3,247 wounded in action
>
> 4,031 TOTAL

Our Division never retreated from any position, we always attacked. Corp ordered us to pull back at Crailsheim and then redirected our attack from the flank, thereby enabling us to deal the enemy severe losses while accomplishing our mission at a minimum loss of lives. This "end run" resulted in our capturing a bridge intact across the Neckar River about 14 km. south of Crailsheim. Upon crossing this bridge, we turned back north and effectively cut off all German reinforcements from the south and west to that beleaguered city. We then turned our attention to the city of Heilbronn.

4
Leadership

Our unit was surrounded on all sides by high, dense hedge rows. We were in the Bocaq Country òf France's Normandy peninsula. One morning we crawled out of our dripping wet two man pup tents. Following a hot breakfast, our troops were ordered to "fall in". After inspection, the order was given to "stand easy". I looked around and noticed at the far end of our field two black and white cows who looked at us with ears forward as if to ask, "Who are these strangers in our grassy meadow?" Suddenly, we were called to attention and in strode front and center none other than General George S. Patton, Commander of the new Third Army. All the things we had heard about him were true. A tall 6'1" man with head erect, chest out, and dressed to perfection — not a wrinkle showing. His helmet liner was polished to a high shine and had a red band in front with three gold stars. On his chest were more medals than I could count. On each hip were his trademarks — two pearl-handled .44 revolvers. His boots shone like his helmet - no mud!

He then began to address us. His rather irritating nasal voice pierced the morning dampness. After welcoming us to the Third Army, he asked if we knew what leadership was. In answer to his own question, he then compared leadership to a plate of spaghetti and a fork. The leader is the fork. If the fork is plunged into the spaghetti and tries to "push" it across the plate, it just bunches up and goes in all directions. But if the fork is used to "pull" the spaghetti across the plate, then the strands easily flow out behind the fork and all the spaghetti moves quickly to the objective with no lost motion. "The fork used properly", he said, "is leadership".

I heard him give this same talk at a later date as well. Both times it struck me as being a good, clear unique example of leadership. In the years to come, I observed this example being lived out on the battlefield many times and at all levels of command.

Now that we understand exactly how leadership works, let us set forth a few examples of it from combat experience:

One of the first examples concerns a certain infantry second lieutenant. He had led his platoon fighting the Nazi, part of last night and all day today, battling the enemy through rain and mud. It was now 1800 hours and dark and he is some place in western France. His company had taken a forested hill just before dark. His men dug in and a hot meal was provided them. They needed it as all were bone tired and wet. To the uninitiated, it must be explained that no fires, nor smoking, nor loud voice nor even talking was allowed. To engage in any of the above would quickly bring down enemy artillery fire upon their heads. So how were these men fed a hot meal? Quite simply. Each platoon sent one squad at a time walking silently to the rear of their company (usually in defilade) where the mess sergeant had his kitchen on the back of a 2-1/2 ton truck, where they ladled out food into each man's mess gear. After a squad had eaten, cleaned, and secured its mess gear, that squad went forward again to its fox holes, receiving ammunition as they went. The next squad was sent for its chow, etc., until the entire company was fed. Once in the fox holes, each man cleaned and checked his individual weapons, hunkered down as best he could and tried to get some shut-eye.

About 2000 hours (8 p.m.), our young second lieutenant began to hear horses snorting "over there" behind the enemy lines. We knew that the Nazi used horse drawn artillery and flat wheeled wagons to haul supplies from the nearest rail-head to their front lines. This was not a bad system as all over Europe one could find a railroad siding and unloading dock in every small village, town, and city. If the proper unloading site was chosen, a division would be no farther away from their front than four or five miles. This process meant about a two hour time frame for delivery of supplies from a loading dock to their front lines. But why were these horses snorting so much? Our puzzled lieutenant rang up his commanding officer and asked him if he heard the snorting. Indeed he had. Our lieutenant asked if he could send a two man patrol to find out what was going on "over there". His captain readily agreed, stipulating that before these men left our lines, the lieutenant must advise him the hour of departure and anticipated time of return, plus the compass course both going out and coming back. This data was to be given to each front line platoon so none of our men would shoot them. The intelligence patrol left at 2100 hours with anticipated return time of 0200 hours the following morning. It was believed that five hours would be sufficient to learn what the enemy intended.

If a mule is overloaded, it "plants" all four feet and will not move until its load is reduced. But when a horse is overloaded, it will try to do what is asked of it but will often snort its disapproval.

About 0200 our patrol returned and located the lieutenant and said, "You would not believe what those Nazis are up to". He said, "Try me". Those Nazis had hitched up a double team of horses to a Panzer tank and pulled it into position behind a hill mask on our front. In fact, with several horse hitches, they had positioned a company of twenty six Panzer tanks there. Their drivers had bedded down on the ground beside their tanks. The exact location of all these tanks was given by our patrol. (The reason horses were used to pull those Panzer tanks forward was to do so in "silence". Had they driven them forward, their engines would have given their location away.) The patrol also located an enemy reserve infantry battalion behind another hill close to the front, obviously intending a surprise tank-infantry attack at dawn.

The lieutenant immediately phoned his commanding officer with this data giving coordinates for each enemy concentration. The captain called his battalion commander who in turn woke up the Combat Commander who quickly woke up the Division Commanding General with this vital information. General Morris then woke up his entire division ordering it to top off their ammo, fuel, get a hot meal and attack with an armored-infantry task force at 0500 hours. This was to be proceeded at 0450 by two "Time-on-Target" artillery barrages, the first on the Panzers and the second on the enemy infantry locations.

Our attack roared off on time and not one of the enemy Panzer tanks was even started. All the tank crews were either killed or wounded while asleep. The same thing happened to the enemy infantry reserve battalion. At 0500 hours and after the two "Time-on-Targets" had been fired, our artillery shifted its fire to the enemy battalion dug in opposite us. Our surprise attack tore through the enemy troop concentrations with minimum loses to our side. This magnificent operation took place because one alert second lieutenant asked the question, "Why were those horses snorting?" and then proceeded to find out. This is true leadership in my opinion and I am sure General Patton's also!

5

Mars LaTour and Metz

After being assigned to Patton's Third U.S. Army, our Division moved out of the Cherbourg area through recently liberated Paris in an easterly direction to the vicinity of the small French village of Mars LaTour.   The village was appropriately named as most battles that rampaged across Europe sooner or later roared through this town. It was here our Division first encountered determined German Army resistance. The "Huns" had pulled out of the French countryside to set up a new line of defense. We attacked them with great vigor.   At that time, I was a forward observer for the Four Hundred Twenty Third Armored Field Artillery Battalion.

Sometime after dark one night, several of us laid out our bed-rolls on the stone floor of a house in Mars LaTour. Lieutenant Colonel Harry B. Feldman, who was our Division's chemical warfare officer, joined us. The Colonel quietly removed all his clothes except his undershorts and slid into his bed-roll. the rest of us removed only our boots before "sacking out", so as to prevent our feet from freezing. As you may know, French farm villagers do not heat their houses. Lieutenant Colonel Feldman must have been very tired as he immediately went to sleep. Shortly thereafter, the farmer's wife, carrying a small child, ran into our room screaming "Vay un! Vay un!" (V-1 Rocket). She was alerting us to an incoming German rocket and pointed to the cellar. Whereupon the good Colonel sat bolt upright, bare from the waist up, (he was a large man with an exceedingly hairy chest), exclaiming in his best French "Madam, have no fear". Immediately he fell backwards to his pillow sound asleep.

The screaming of the woman plus our Colonel's ludicrous action woke us all. Several of us ran to the front door; looking out, we could see a dark large cigar-shaped rocket with blue flame belching from its rear.

It was traveling due west, about one hundred fifty feet above us and paralleling "our street". We watched as it traveled out of town and then a "surprise"! It did a one hundred eighty degree turn retracing its path back over our street and out of town to the east. A short time later we heard a huge blast in the German held territory. I thought, "Hurray for those slave laborers who had programmed into this rocket such a "defect" to thwart their German masters. "Score one for freedom!", for this sabotaged action.

The next day or two saw fierce combat. After pushing the Nazi line back, our Division plunged southward accompanying the main body of the Third Army to prepare and then attack Metz in Alsace-Lorraine. Before proceeding with that great battle, some of our tanks were sent still farther south to back up other U.S. troops in the Colmar Pocket, which amounted to auxiliary side action but did lend us some additional experience.

Some of our tanks and artillery were to thicken the fires of friendly U.S. troops already there. For our artillery it was easy, except for the terribly cold weather. To make matters worse, all farm houses had been destroyed in 1940 by attacking Germans and none had been repaired in the intervening three years. The temperature hovered about ten degrees F. and was accompanied by a cold wind from nearby Swiss alpine glaciers.

Our tanker officers had at one point or another in their army training been exposed to "laying their tanks for indirect fire". As few of them had ever done so and to prevent our tanks from shooting friendly infantry, several artillery officers were ordered to assist them in "indirect fire". I was one of them, and it proved to be a very interesting operation. We helped the armored troops to lay and fire many rounds which enhanced the front line infantry division's artillery fire. In spite of the bitterly cold weather this effort took only two or three days as nearly as I can recall. We were all mighty glad to move back north to invest and attack Metz.

The ancient city of Metz was surrounded by a great wall with medieval turrets and gates. The wall was not fortified, however. The city was situated on a flat plain with a small stream running through the town. Surrounding Metz, were six large steep-sided granite hills which rose about sixty feet above the plain. Over the centuries, these hills had been fortified to such an extent that no army had ever successfully overcome these six forts. Truly, the Metz area, including these forts, had changed hands many times, but always as a result of treaties or military victories won elsewhere, never by direct assault. Each time these fortified hills "changed hands", the most recent victor added several feet of wall thickness to them.

Fort Driant was the largest and toughest of the six. It was the headquarters and nerve center where artillery from all six were directed against an approaching enemy. The telephone lines to the other forts had been buried deep underground so they were free from destruction by an attacking army. With such a high observation level, an approaching enemy could be spotted miles away. Fort Driant was therefore singled out for the Corp attack. Two infantry divisions hit it from the front and our Tenth Armored Division was to encircle it and come up from the rear. Preceding all of this ground action, our Air Force tactical wing strafed and bombed it. Their bombs helped the ground forces as the fourteen foot thick walls of Fort Driant were breeched in several placed. Our heavy air attack also killed and wounded many of its defenders. All this action did not make it a "push-over" for us, however, since it was obviously strongly defended.

Two very vivid memories stand out for me. The first one I recall was sitting astride the radiator of our half-track and hanging onto the vertical post wire cutter with which all our vehicles were equipped. (This part was welded and braced to the half-track's front bumper). It was a dark, moonless night and our Division was moving up under orders of total black-out and radio silence. The night was dark due to intermittent cloud cover which allowed only a little starlight. Thus our driver could not see the ditch on each side of the secondary road, and we were traveling slowly as he could barely make out the vehicle twenty feet ahead of us. I volunteered to sit on the radiator peering from side to side. When our half-track came near to the right ditch, I would call out "left" and vice versa, so our driver was aided in keeping us on the road. The only reason I could see the ditches was the water in them which served a mirrors reflecting the faint starlight overhead.

We traveled for some miles in first gear as our armored

columns stretched for several miles ahead and behind us as well as on other roads parallel to us, all vehicles were creeping up slowly and as quietly as possible for the pending "kill". All of a sudden without warning, a 240 mm. battery about fifty feet to my right opened up. The blast nearly knocked me off the radiator to say nothing of the bright hang-fire at the muzzle. We had no idea of the presence of this Corp Artillery. This was the beginning of our softening-up process on Fort Driant.

If you have never had the experience of being near the heavy artillery (8" or 240 mm. howitzer) when they fire, you have really missed a show! I recall, as a young lad, a neighbor across the street at home telling me he had been in the A.E.F. in France during World War I. Even though he was in the supply section several miles back, he claimed that he could sit outside and read a newspaper any night from heavy gun flashes. I really didn't believe him. But this night outside of Fort Driant, I saw for myself that it was possible, because when those heavies fired, a brilliant hang-fire flared at their muzzles for several seconds. When shells exploded "over there", their burst also had a very bright hang-fire. A battery of heavies consisted of two Howitzers and a battalion consisted of six. As each fired, the staggered hang-fire here plus the staggered hang-fire of the shell explosion reflected so much light off the underside of the cloud cover, that the entire "front" was as bright as day. Immediately all our armored columns speeded up and began to launch the attack, and, of course, the Nazi defenders opened up on us as well. I hastily retreated inside our half-track.

The second recollection of the Metz battle was when the "team" for which I was F.O. charged over the threshold of Fort

Driant, through lots of smoke and fire. Dead Germans were laying all about. The live ones were still shooting at us with small arms from within the inner defenses of the Fort. This did not last long as our men quickly rounded up all the enemy.

Two things forcefully struck me. First were those fourteen foot thick walls of this Fort. Each succeeding "owner" had added to them. One could clearly see the original rock formation from which this defensive position had been dug or blasted. The original rock walls were about four feet thick. Next was a layer of brick and mortar about six feet thick. Lastly was the most recent layer of four feet of steel reinforced concrete which had been added by the Germans more recently.

The second thing that I noticed was that the defenders had killed their artillery horses and had cut steaks from these animals and eaten them to sustain themselves. For the very first time, I realized that many Europeans enjoyed eating horse flesh, and some areas considered it a true delicacy. These Germans had no choice as our Division had cut off all their supplies and they ate what was available. This was the first time any army had successfully attacked and captured Fort Driant and the other five fortified hills in warfare.

6

Down Wind from Trouble

In 1944 when our Division was fighting the rear guard action of Hitler's minions in the vicinity of Mars LaTour, France, I was ordered back to the Four Hundred Twenty Third Armored Field Artillery Battalion Headquarters from my forward observer post.

All of us were trying to take short cuts in those days to save time. Reviewing my map, I noticed what appeared to be a good secondary road cutting through a wooded area. There was a symbol about half way through this area showing the location of permanent French barracks. As we were allies with the French, I never gave it a second thought and directed my jeep driver toward this location. Actually, I figured this short cut would save several miles as compared to circumventing this large wooded are via the main road; so off we went.

As this road entered the wooded area, about the first thing which attracted our attention was a deserted wood cutter's or forester's house. Its windows were broken out and the door creaked as the wind battered it on its rusty hinges; this seemed odd. Next, railroad tracks appeared alongside the road next to the house. The railroad bed seemed in good condition but both rails were rusted which indicated little or no recent use. This caused us no particular concern either.

Suddenly, we rounded a small curve and there on our right stood the French barracks! You may remember that all such French posts were surrounded by twelve to fourteen foot high stone walls and large double gates that allowed entry into an inner courtyard. Here we stopped the jeep as our road turned right directly through a large gate into the post. The railroad continued on for sixty yards or so to a long loading dock which backed up to a row of freight sheds.

My driver slowly turned into the front gate of the compounds expecting to be greeted by "challenge". But no one was there so we hollered and called out again - still no answer. We both jumped from our jeep and opened several barrack doors and even investigated the freight sheds. The place was deserted. All the rooms were still furnished just as if troops were expected back momentarily. This was not the case, however, as at least a half inch of dust covered all tables, chairs, and desks. No troops had been billeted there for several years, or so it appeared. An eerie feeling came upon as as if French soldiers' spirits were peering at us but we could not see them.

We quickly concluded that for us to be at Battalion Headquarters in timely fashion, we had better drive out the rear gate and be on our way along the secondary road. We had not driven far, when suddenly we discovered that this entire wooded area was a French chemical warfare site. On both sides of our road were U-shaped reverts now grass covered. Facing our road between them were six, eight inch, and 240 mm. artillery shells and 1000 kg. bombs from World War I. The nose cones of each round or bomb were clearly marked with the symbol for phosgene or mustard gas. The O.D. paint on some of these old World War I shells and bombs was getting dull due to oxidation and weathering. But bombs and shells produced and stored from the 1930's had a much brighter shine to their O.D. paint. We noticed that a few of the older bombs showed clear signs of deterioration, i.e. paint blisters, indicating their steel shells were rusting through from the inside. It would only be a short time before these bombs would begin to "leak" their deadly cargo into the atmosphere.

Other roads ran off this main road at regular right angles and these also had large shells and bombs stacked in U-shaped redoubts or open earth works. These shells were stacked in pyramids of ten; four on the bottom, then three, then two, and one on top. The bombs, however, were stacked by three; two on the bottom and one on the top.

When the realization sank in that we were in the middle of a chemical storage site, both my driver and I searched for our gas masks. He could not find his and mine had a broken strap so it was useless. Next, we had a strong and sudden desire to be gone from this place. All Heinie would have to do would be to lop an H.E. shell into this area and we would be in deep, deep trouble. I can tell you quite frankly, we turned tail and hiked out of this place at once, returning to the route we had come. Both of us agreed that the time lost going around these woods via the main road was well worth it!

It became obvious to me that after Hitler destroyed the French army and forced the British out of Dunkirk in May and June, 1940, he controlled what was left of French fighting forces by gaining control of France politically. Naturally the French were not allowed to garrison many of their former posts, including the one we so recently visited. Hitler did not really care if a few old French chemical warfare bombs and shells leaked their deadly poison gas. Prevailing winds from this dump blew directly toward a few small French farming villages less than three miles distance. Should a few farm animals and French families be killed or maimed, Hitler could care less.

So you see this really was a case of these villages being "down wind — from trouble".

7
Mystery at Division Headquarters

The question has often been asked of me, "How does one become a general's aide?". I don't know. Next question: "What does an aide do?". At first I didn't know either.

Let's begin at the start. I had been a Forward Observer for the Four Hundred Twenty Third Armored Field Artillery Battalion until 12 December, 1944. At that time our Division was at Apach, France. Colonel Beverly, the Four Hundred Twenty Third Armored Field Artillery Battalion Commander told me to report at 1000 hours to Colonel Thayer at Division Headquarters; no reason or explanation was given. Because Colonel Thayer was Chief of Division Staff and an important officer, I decided to shape up a little, so I cleaned mud off my boots and pants and polished my brass with a borrowed blitz cloth.

When I arrived at Division Headquarters, I saw twenty other second lieutenants. We were asking one another what this was all about, but no one knew. Later I found out that Colonel Thayer required each battalion in our Division to send one officer for an interview. One at a time each of us reported to the Colonel and after some questions were asked we were dismissed and told to return to our units. We still did not know any more than before.

The next morning in the 423rd officer's mess, Colonel Beverly introduced me as the new aide to General Morris. I was truly thunder-struck; it was the furthest thing from my mind at that moment. So on 13 December, 1944, I reported first to Colonel Thayer and then was introduced to General Morris.

Afterwards, I went to Colonel Thayer when he was free, and asked him what I was supposed to do as an aide. He gave me a few pointers and added, "You do whatever the General wishes you to do. You are his right hand man."

Had I been told to lead an infantry platoon, or a tank platoon, I could have done so, but perhaps with some uncertainty as I had been through both basic infantry training and our division's tank training courses. I would have felt quite at home in an artillery spot. As an aide to a general officer I was scared silly.

The next morning, I went to Division officers' mess early. There were only a couple of lieutenants and a captain there eating at a back table. The head table was marked for the general and Colonel Thayer. I recalled my Sunday school lesson as a boy where Christ was trying to educate his rough and ready followers as to social niceties. He said when you are invited to a dinner do not go and sit at the right hand of the host at the head table, but rather sit at the foot of the table for if you sit at the place of honor and the host asked you to move because he wishes another to be honored, then you will be embarrased. But if the host comes to you at the foot of the table and invites you to sit in the seat of honor by him you will be honored indeed. So I sat down with the two lieutenants at the rear table. The mess filled up rapidly with field grade officers and captains. Soon the General and Colonel Thayer came in and sat down at the head table. The Colonel spotted me at the back table and came over and invited me to come and sit with General Morris and him. I was honored to say the least! That was to be my regular spot from then on, I was told.

At the conclusion of our breakfast, Colonel Thayer stood up to command everyone's attention and introduced me as the General's new aide. Without hesitation all these officers came over and introduced themselves, warmly greeted me and made me fell welcome. As a result, I was nearly speechless. Military courtesy was required in any such change but it was obvious that my greeting went far beyond this requisite. Afterwards I expressed my astonishment to Colonel Thayer; he only smiled and said, "Some day you may understand." A week later I understood!

At division level a general officer has two aides per tables of organization. The senior aide is a social one while the junior aide is the tactical one. During my time with General Morris in the division, I was his only aide. When he was promoted after combat to VI Corp Commander, he brought up from our Division Major George Signeous to be his senior aide and I became his junior aide. This arrangement suited me fine as George was a natural politician and I didn't care about such matters. By nature I am not a jealous person and so all concerned were happy with this arrangement.

In combat the General used me in several ways. Often he would send me up to one combat command while he went to the other. My job was to observe how our units functioned under fire and how well the unit commanders carried out their orders, and also I must check on any supply shortages. The one thing an aide must never do is to "wear a general's stars". I could give no orders to senior or field grade officers as I was a staff member only and woe to an aide who did not remember this role. I had the right to ask questions of any unit officer or commander but they were usually so busy I tried not to bother them. Any information I felt was needed could usually be obtained from a junior staff member of those units any time or at a later hour from a senior officer. Should something appear amiss, I would certainly report it as soon as possible to the General.

At every river crossing or other major bottle neck, General Morris required my immediate presence to observe, since he often arrived later to see for himself. Whenever our Division was to pass through a regular infantry division, I usually was at the point of pass through to observe and/or carry messages.

If an order had to be changed to a combat commander and if the General felt a radio message was too risky, I carried the message forward. Some of these adventures were hair raising, especially driving at night through wooded areas with accompanying tree bursts from artillery.

As a general rule, I managed no more than three hours of sleep per night. This lack of sleep caused me severe headaches, an after several weeks of this I felt punchy. It seems as if my mind functioned in slow motion while my body felt "disconnected" and slow to respond. One of the toughest things I had to do was to commit to memory all enemy unit locations and mine fields as well as our task force disposition route and mine fields. A map could be carried forward of Division Headquarters but no details or markings were allowed on it. Should this map fall into enemy hands, they would not learn anything that they did not already know. When one realizes our Division often fought and moved twenty miles a day and shifted directions rapidly, a good alert memory was certainly required. At one point I remember I did not remove my clothes nor have a bath for six weeks, so it was certainly good we had cold weather. I tried to shave every day by simply removing my tie, and removed my boots and socks for daily massage of my feet with G.I. foot powder to prevent trench foot. Naturally, I pulled the same dirty old wool socks back on again.

In addition, I taught the General's two staff sergeants to ridge and stream line maps for him. At various times I was responsible for upwards of thirty-four men, not in the administrative sense, but in combat and tactical matters. Most of these men were N.C.O.'s and specialists of various kinds. The General had for his use three medium tanks, two half-tracks, two jeeps, and two armored cars. When our Division was issued the new light tank mounting the 75 mm. gun, he replaced all three medium tanks and the old light tanks for two new light tanks. All of these were especially useful as they had all sixteen radio channels.

I was required to write letters for the General's signature as well as research and write some of the citations which he bestowed upon men and officers of the Division. One particular letter stands out from all the rest. Returning late one evening dog tired, and a little jumpy from all the enemy artillery tree bursts along my route, he handed me a letter and asked me to frame an answer for his signature. This letter and envelope were of cheap quality; the type one used to be able to purchase in a dime store. Its handwriting was crude and the diction even worse. It was a letter addressed to the "Commanding Officer of our Division" - no name and no title. It seemed this dear mother had not heard from her son, Joe, for over two months. She did not give Joe's full name or rank or serial number or unit, merely stated that he was in our Division. It was a cry of an anguished mother pleading to hear from her Joe and fearful something had happened to him.

From her name and return address and the poor grammar, I concluded she was foreign born, poorly educated, but a loving mother. Without any more data about her son, where was I to begin? Taking pen in hand I made out a buck slip to our personnel section stating that the General wished to answer this letter. We needed more information about who Joe was and his name and unit. Clipping this to her letter, I sent it to the personnel division at rear headquarters. It did not seem to me there would be a prayer of a chance to find "Joe" among 17,600 men and officers of our Division.

A few days later to my surprise an answer was returned to me. Someone did a lot of detective work on this. Making a mental note, I stopped by Joe's infantry squad next day asking about him. Yes, Joe was a private in their squad and a good soldier. While his squad was attacking a Kraut strong point two months earlier, a shell burst near Joe, killing him instantly. Later that night I dictated the reply for General Morris' signature to the affect that her Joe was a brave and excellent soldier, a credit to free Americans everywhere and especially our Division. We deeply regretted to have to inform her of his death while charging an enemy machine gun, but death had come quickly and without pain. Tears still come to my eyes when I think about this mother reading the General's letter.

She would not receive his letter in all probability for another two months. All such correspondence and personal effects were required by army regulations to go directly to Kansas City, Kansas to the Army's burial and graves registration section. They would be released to her only after the usual War Department telegram was sent telling of her son's death.

8
A Star Falls

Many of you will recall our short stay in Teurtheville-Bocage which is a small rural town on the Cherbourg peninsula of France. You may also remember the middle-aged village schoolmaster of that town, Monsieur F. Gilles. I can almost hear him now speaking flawless English with a decidedly British accent. M. Gilles had been married in the early 1930's and his son was about eight years old at the time of our arrival. Our Combat Command A under General Kenneth Althaus had taken over the town. Immediately M. Gilles offered General Althaus and the Americans his services as an interpreter and guide. His son could already speak fluent French and German and within the next few weeks he learned to talk like an American G.I.

M. Gilles was greatly impressed by General Althaus and considered him one of the finest gentlemen and officers with which he had ever worked. For many years after the war I corresponded with this most excellent schoolmaster, and in so doing we became fast friends. He always concluded his letters by telling me to give his best regards to General Althaus. Unfortunately, I could not do so as General Althaus left our Division just before our preparation to attack the Switch Position of the Siegfried Line. I lost track of the good General. Since the mid 1940's, I also have lost track of M. Gilles. Time and distance has a way of separating us all.

Nearly fifty years now separate General Althaus'

departure from our Division as Combat Command A Commander. I believe it is now time to record the full reason for his unfortunate leaving. I am certain by this time all the principal actors of this situation have "gone to their reward", so now it is time to lift a curtain of secrecy.

Unknown to anyone, beginning with our first footfalls on French soil in 1944, Brigadier General K.G. Althaus began experiencing pains of arthritis in his shoulders and arms. He did not complain and for two or three months did not even see his Combat Command A doctor. All this time his pain became more and more acute. It became so bad that he could sleep only a few minutes at a time. He began to pace the floor and tried to kill this ever intensifying pain by taking handfuls of aspirin (P.A.C.'s) gulped down with increasing quantities of brandy and whiskey. The pain was almost unbearable but he never complained nor spared himself in the line of duty. Gradually his staff began to realize his serious condition. His attempted cure and the accumulated lack of sleep left him "punchy" and drawn. His staff greatly respected and admired their general as did all the enlisted men and officers who knew or had occasion to work with him. He was one of my favorites as well. What happened next to him was painful to all of us.

His staff finally and sadly concluded that something must be done. They were afraid that due to his increasing pain, lack of sleep and rest, and the increasing amounts of alcohol he consumed, he might misjudge a situation, thereby putting his troops at tragic risk. What to do? Finally they drew straws and the one having the short straw was to go to General Morris and explain the situation and their fears for the Combat Command

A Command.

As I recall this incident, a lieutenant colonel arrived about dusk one night and asked to see General Morris. He was duly ushered into the Commanding General's office which was a room in an old house. The door was closed and this officer, as representative of our Combat Command A's staff, told General Morris their concern. He also requested that General Althaus not be told about their staff action and to keep his name secret. The lieutenant colonel regretted having to make this report to General Morris. The staff felt extremely sad as they had the greatest respect for General Althaus and there was certainly nothing he had done to deserve his dreadful arthritic pains. It was just one of those events of life which none of us can control.

General Morris heard the lieutenant colonel out and readily agreed to keep their secret from General Althaus. General Morris waited awhile that evening to give the staff officers time to return to duty at Combat Command A Headquarters. Then he phoned to General Althaus to come at once to Division Headquarters where he questioned him behind closed doors as to the truth of the situation.

General Althaus agreed on all counts and admitted he too had feared secretly of making an error under these conditions which could jeopardize his troops. Within that hour, Brigadier General Piburn was transferred to the Command of Combat Command A from Combat Command B and Colonel W.L. (Robby) Roberts was elevated to the Command of Combat Command B. Absolute silence clothed this entire episode with the exception that General Piburn and Colonel Roberts were given detailed explanations. At the same time they and a few of us were cautioned not even to talk about this. Out of deep respect for General Althaus, to my knowledge, this confidence has been tightly held all these intervening years. But now the story should be told in fairness to General K.G. Althaus and others concerned.

He was a great and able commander, a true gentlemen in every way, and a good friend to all. No greater tribute can be given to mortal man. As M. Gilles so often wrote, "Give my best regards to General Althaus.".

9
Switch Position — Siegfried Line

If one were to draw a triangle with its apex at Trier which is at the confluence of the Saar and Moselle rivers, the base of this triangle would be due east and west between these two rivers; resulting in an equal angle triangle approximately seventeen miles on a side. The two sides of the triangle would be the two rivers.

Across the base of this geographic triangle, the Nazi's had built in 1939 a switch position of their western wall or as we called it, the Siegfried Line. The ends of this "base" were anchored at each river. The "line" itself consisted of the longest, deepest tank trap I have ever seen, measuring seventeen miles long, forty feet deep and about forty feet wide. In front was a military barbed wire concertina, which also stretched seventeen miles from one river to the other. In between the wire and dragon's teeth were buried camouflaged Teller tank mines. Ahead of the wire were anti-personnel mines called "shoe box mines" or "bouncing bets", so named for their characteristic of springing up fourteen inches and then exploding at knee level destroying the legs of enemy soldiers. These nasty little devils were set off by a soldier barely touching their camouflaged trip wire.

Behind all of this was the Nazi's main line of defense consisting of pill boxes with interlocking fire and gun emplacements all adequately camouflaged, of course. These pill boxes and gun emplacements were constructed of reinforced concrete and steel. All together this switch position, as well as the rest of German's west wall or Siegfried Line, was considered a very formidable defense work. Its camouflage was especially effective, and was now augmented by four years of undisturbed growth of natural vines and vegetation.

Now for our assault on the switch position. Having discovered the anti-personnel mine fields ahead of the military wire, we simply ran several heavy tanks back and forth over the mine area thus exploding the shoe boxes under them harmlessly. Of course the Nazi defenders pelted our tanks with heavy fire, and thus gave away their gun emplacements, enabling our tanks and artillery to zero in immediately on their defenses.

Our engineers and infantry cut the barbed wire and pulled sections of wire out of place to allow access or routes for forward movement of our infantry and tanks. Due to the heavy machine gun fire and mortar fire over the mine fields, our infantry fell back taking cover and the engineers went through gaps in the wire to remove the Teller mines. If there had been no fire from the enemy, mine detectors would have been used. Because of the incoming heavy machine gun and mortar fire, our men lay flat against the earth and inched slowly forward shoulder to shoulder using bayonets or hunting knives to push into the ground in an endeavor to locate the tank mines. When one was found, a charge was laid above it and everyone pulled back allowing the mine to be blown. Afterward, a line of men then moved forward again to locate more mines.

In addition to our men being hit by enemy fire, there was

another danger. These Teller mines were set off by a wire spider attached to the detonator. If an engineer soldier shoved his knife into the ground with too much force and hit one of these spiders, it could also detonate a mine nearly below his head. The result was not only lethal to that man but usually it killed one or two soldiers on both sides of him as well.

After our men had pushed part way through various mine fields, our Division was ordered out of the Saar-Mosell Triangle and sent north by General Patton to strike the southern flank of Von Rundstedt's attack at Bastogne.   This encounter is described elsewhere.

10
Stretchers

After Brigadier General Althaus was evacuated to the hospital, General Piburn was transferred from Combat Command B and given Command of Combat Command A. General Piburn was of medium height, very agile and had iron grey hair and a neatly trimmed moustache. His high cheek bones and piercing black eyes indicated he had some Indian blood. From our very first meeting, I instantly liked and trusted him. His neat appearance and agile mind enforced this impression of him. He brought with him a Lieutenant Taylor as his aide, a pleasant young officer.

General Piburn had commanded our Combat Command A only a short time in combat when Major General Morris, our Division Commander, accompanied by me, decided to check the progress that Combat Command A was making in their attacks. One day General Morris' jeep was leading General Piburn's by some fifty yards on a secondary dirt road. General Morris decided that we should turn around and go back to the last cross road and take a different route. Our driver made an immediate U-turn and General Piburn's driver started to do the same at almost the exact spot where we had turned. (I looked at these tracks later; there was not more than one half inch difference in them.)

General Piburn's jeep hit a land mine at that turning point. The jeep somersaulted skyward and came down upon its driver, killing him instantly. General Piburn was thrown clear of the jeep and slammed against a tree breaking his arm and some ribs. The blast also damaged both ear drums. Lieutenant Taylor, his aide, was sitting in the rear seat with his right foot on the side rail. The chop of the blast sheared off his right leg just above the ankle and threw him clear of the jeep.

We immediately stopped and gave first aid while calling for the medics who promptly responded. A few days later General Morris and I went to the field hospital to visit our fallen friends.

In the meantime who should be reassigned to us as General Piburn's replacement, but Colonel Thayer. Such are the fortunes of war! He had been our Division Chief of Staff until the time he was wounded by shell fire at our Division's Command Post at Ayl, Germany.

11
Cold Sweat and Hot Flashes

Those of you who were there will recall vividly our hair-raising move north from the switch position of the Siegfried Line into and through Luxembourg City to back up the Fourth Infantry on the eastern edge of Luxembourg.

The main road to the north went through Nancy, Metz, Luxembourg City, and Bastogne. It was a crowned black-top road, ice covered and so our steel belted vehicles slid off frequently. Additionally, total black-out and radio silence prevailed. All of these added to our difficulty moving through a very black night with snow squalls, a heavy overcast sky and fog.

This main road crossed twelve bridges just south of Luxembourg City. As this area had many ravines, these bridges did not cross over streams or rivers but rather over deep and jagged crevasses and ravines. The Germans guessed correctly that Patton would try to send his army northward over these bridges to attack their salient's flank. As we were passing over these bridges on the early morning of 17-18 December, 1944, the Nazis began to shell them with a "Big Bertha" (12.8") located on a railway car some twenty miles to the east. They really did not know of our Division's movement at the time. It was several hours later when we hit them through Fourth Infantry positions that the German Fifth Army first learned of our move from the switch position of the Siegfried Line to Luxembourg proper.

At the time of this shelling, I was crossing these bridges. They were beautiful limestone structures with supporting arches beneath each one. Our column moved very slowly and so it took considerable time to cross all of them. I recall when that first shell whined over us, it sounded so low overhead that I believed I could literally reach up and touch it. The shell then exploded with a terrible roar some two hundred yards down range. As each shell whined overhead, my stomach knotted, my breathing stopped, as well as my heart. Then came the roar, always down range. As an artillery officer, this roar told me that the Huns were firing from map data and not observed fire, for if they had been, their second round would have been short and then they would have split the bracket. Of course, I was thankful that it was not observed fire. In spite of how fired, each and every time one of those large rounds whined overhead, my reaction was the same; knotted stomach, hard breathing and heart stopped. Then after the explosion down range came relief, so another two minutes of life were allowed us. To say that my hands and body were bathed with "cold sweat" and only relieved by the "hot flash" and explosion down range was only too true. Others must have felt the same, I presume.

The only real physical damage incurred by this action was the destruction of a lime stone government office building and statuary in a wooded park-like setting down range from those bridges. One of those shells weighed half as much as a Volkswagen.

It should be pointed out that had any one of those bridges been hit, they would have been very difficult to replace as there was no water upon which to float a replacement pontoon bridge.

After having cleared these bridges, the scary feeling of being hit by 12.8" shells quickly passed and we continued on to the Fourth Infantry Division's area. It was here that General Morris met General "Stub" Barton who was the Commanding General of the Fourth. When these two old friends from West Point days saw each other, General "Stub" Barton threw his arms around General "Bill" Morris exclaiming, "Boy am I glad to see you!" Then the two danced a jig for joy at meeting once again. For more details of their joint effort see the chapter "Bastogne".

General Barton took us into his headquarters showing us his division's situation map. In the words of Lieutenant Colonel Shefield, our G-3, it looked as if it had measles, with the "blue" of enemy troop perforating the "red" of friendly forces. General Morris immediately directed our Combat Command A and Combat Command R to stop the hemorrhage and clean out the draws through which the enemy was infiltrating the Fourth Infantry's positions. For the next seven to ten days and nights, our two Combat Commands carried out their tasks. At first our Combat Command B was held in a reserve status for our Division. On 18 December, 1944, Combat Command B was ordered to Bastogne - another story!

12
Bastogne — Out of the Fog

To be a truly great battle two attributes are required: First, it must be fought against overwhelming odds and one side must be a clear winner. Second, the outcome must affect not only that war but also the course of history for at least fifty years. Our Tenth Armored Division's battle at Bastogne satisfied both of these criteria.

Answers to two questions are of interest:

1st - Does God influence the actions of men in war?

2nd - If so, how?

The weather from 20 November through 23 December, 1944 was terrible for our troops in the Bastogne-Luxembourg area. There was solid cloud cover continually with the exception of a two hour break about noon on 22 December. After Patton's celebrated prayer for good weather at daybreak on 23 December, the skies cleared completely. Most of this time temperatures ranged from the low teens to mid 20's F. About daylight on the 20th, the temperature rose to 30 degrees F. for only a few hours. Then it plunged again.

During the calm periods, fog shrouded the entire area from 0100 hours until usually 1100 hours. Occasionally it snowed heavily with driving winds and sleet, and at other times there were just flurries and fog. Snow was five inches deep by 23 December. Back in the U.S.A., H.V. Kaltenborn on his nightly news cast declared, "Your boys are cold tonight in

Europe", and we sure were! It was so frigid, fog chilled one to the marrow of his bones. As a matter of fact, whenever a soldier died, he "froze" instantly in his final posture. Patton's staff reported that when Patton saw these frozen bodies in their bizarre postures, he wept. [1]

Prior to the invasion of "D" Day, the English had broken the German code, and showed us how this feat was accomplished. Before our men hit the beaches, the Allies knew troop locations, orders, commanders, military strengths, troop assembly points, and reserve strengths. In short, we knew everything about the Germans right down to their "dirty socks".

By early November 1944, however, the entire German Army in the west was just a few kilometers outside of the Fatherland or actually on its own frontier. Hence they reverted to telephones and messengers in lieu of radio. It so happened that on 23 November, 1944, one lone O.S.S. spy was able to crawl through the German lines and inform the First U.S. Army that the Germans were assembling a large tank force at Frankfort, Germany.

Our army has a policy that whenever one source makes such a statement it is labeled a rumor and is immediately communicated as such to all units with the request to attempt to verify it. If it could be verified by a different source, then all units were so notified and prompt action would be taken. In this instance, no one was able to verify the rumor by an independent source, so it was ignored by all U.S. and Allied generals except Patton.

On or about 27 November, 1944, General Eisenhower issued an order to all units to halt in place and dig in or fortify

[1] Patton, Ordeal and Triumph by Lodisios Fargo

their lines because it was his belief, along with that of the British and French, that the Germans could <u>not</u> mount an attack until the weather cleared and warmed as estimated to occur about the end of February 1945. General Patton, upon receiving this order was reported to have told his staff that his Third Army would <u>not</u> dig in nor wire nor mine, but would attack instead; and attack he did! Being "Army smart", he had his staff refer to all such actions as "a reconnaissance in force"!

On 1 December, 1944, during one of Patton's staff meetings, he declared that the rumored build up of German armor at Frankfort was probably the precursor of a massive German attack. He posed three questions to his staff: (1) Where would it take place? (2) When would it be? (3) How large would it be?

Patton and his staff rolled up their sleeves and spent the remainder of that day working on these hypothetical questions. They determined after studying the entire front from the English Channel to Switzerland, that the Germans would launch their attack from the Ardennes Forest just as they did in May, 1940 against the French and English, and for the same reasons. The Ardennes is a large, heavily wooded, roughly terrained area with only two track roads similar to National Forest areas in Northern Michigan. Thousands of troops and tanks and guns can be hidden in this area prior to a surprise attack. This forest area happened to be opposite the First U.S. Army area.

Next, estimating the time it would take to move such a large mass of troops, the investigation came up with the earliest possible date of 15 December. Third, by searching all known estimates of enemy strength, it was believed that no larger force could be hurled at the First Army than 100,000 men and tanks.

How accurate were these estimates? The location they guessed exactly. The date of mid-December or the 15th was short by only two hours! But the estimate of the size of the attacking force was very wrong. The reason for this bad estimate was that the Germans reduced their Russian front's troops, contrary to current beliefs, and moved their best divisions and officers to General Von Rundstedt's offensive, so their actual force was 250,000 men, artillery and tanks — the most Germany could muster. There were more experienced divisions and better units, including Air Force, in Von Rundstedt's force than on the entire Russian front after the transfers.

In 1939, just prior to the treaty made by Germany and Russia to partition Poland, Stalin became concerned about loyalty of his top army staff, so he had them all executed. This act literally de-capitated his armed forces' leadership, and greatly reduced morale and resulted in slip-shod training in the armed forces. The Germans knew about this purge. Additionally, Stalin paid the Germans with gold and oil as part of his bargain to split up Poland. When the Germans actually invaded Russia, troops opposing them were poorly trained and equipped. Furthermore, several thousand Ukrainians gladly joined the German Army to fight against Stalin due to Stalin's earlier starvation policy of Ukrainian farmers as they had refused to work on Russia's collective farms. Hence, the German general staff believed they had nothing to fear from Russia and so reduced that front to bolster General Von Rundstedt's efforts.

The German plan was a classic blitzkrieg scheme of maneuvering. The Sixth Panzer S.S. Army was to seize the important road center of Malmedy, cross the Meuse River, and move on to Antwerp. The Seventh Panzer S.S. Army was to follow in trace its Sixth Panzer Army. The Fifth Panzer Army was to seize the vital road centers of St. Vith, Houffalize and Bastogne, cross the Meur River, and then turn north to Antwerp. These armies included ten tank and fourteen infantry divisions. The Germans went to great lengths to keep secret their offensive plans. Extreme preparations were carried out, i.e. furnishing all their infantry white tunics to go over their field grey uniforms and to paint all trucks and tanks white so that they all would blend into the snow covering the ground.

The Germans envisioned that this attack would destroy the First U.S. Army and capture Antwerp, thereby cutting off the Ninth Army and General Montgomery's British Army from the rest of the allied forces. Their Panzers would then destroy the Ninth American and the British Armies. Their scheme almost worked!

In late October or early November, 1944, "Ike" had ordered Monty (General Montgomery) to attack Antwerp and take its sea port, since the Allies had need of this facility to supply its armies. Eventually Monty did capture the port, but he neglected to seize several small fortified islands and a Dutch peninsula at its mouth. As long as the Germans held these, no Allied vessel could enter the Port of Antwerp. The Germans resupplied these islands under cover of darkness via submarines and high speed patrol boats.

This oversight was not lost upon the German High

Command, however, which decreed that those islands would be the "anvil" and Von Rundstedt's offensive the "hammer".

The geographic area for our consideration is that of the country of Luxembourg and the southern Belgium area. The terrain of eastern Luxembourg was unique, geographically speaking. This area was faulted with hinges of various faults running east and west or at approximately ninety degrees to the existing north-south rivers. Each fault, from hinge to fractured cliff face, varied from four to six hundred yards and covered about half the eastern side of this small country. These faults were heavily forested with pine trees, and there were no roads or foot trails through them. During this time, these pine trees were heavily laden with snow.

The initial thrust of Von Rundstedt's offensive had his Sixth Panzer S.S. Army attacking the northern half of First U.S. Army. The Seventh S.S. Panzer followed it in trace, while his Fifth Regular Panzer Army attacked the southern half of First U.S. Army. During the first two days, the Sixth Panzer Army destroyed one regiment of the U.S. One Hundred Sixth Infantry Division. Unfortunately, the other two regiments of that Division surrendered, leaving a gaping hole in First U.S. Army's front lines through which the German Sixth and Seventh Armies poured.

The Fifth Panzer Army was commanded by General H. Monteuffel, and under his command was General H. Luttwitz, the Forty Seventh Corp Commanding General. The three divisions which comprised this leading corp were the Second Panzer Division under Colonel Lauchert, the Twenty Sixth Volks-Grenadier Infantry Division under General H. Kokott and the Panzer-Lear Division under General F. Bayerlein. These were the best regular Army Divisions the Germans had anywhere. All three Divisions had extensive combat experience in either western or eastern Europe or both. Their "Schwerpunkt" or main effort was: "Objective Bastogne!". In the first forty eight hours the German's Fifth Army had marked seven areas to be taken in their attack: St. Vith, four crossings of the Meusse River, the high ground north and east of Bastogne, and Bastogne itself. The first six fell within their time frame, but not Bastogne. Bastogne was very critical to their needs because it was the highway and rail center needed to move supplies west and then north to support their three Panzer armies.

General H. Monteuffel disguised himself as a colonel and walked his front lines for three to four weeks prior to his attack. He discovered by observation and nightly patrols inside the First Army's lines that the American One Hundred Sixth and the Twenty Eighth Infantry Divisions were scattered and had gaps between and within units. Also, the Fourth Infantry Division had been in the Hurtgen Forest and, while having won that battle, they had lost half their forces. The Fourth had been stretched out over a forty mile perimeter along the eastern edge of Luxembourg and just in front of those faults previously mentioned. The Combat Command R of the Ninth Armored Division had never been in combat and had just been put into the line 7 December. In addition, the Combat Command R Ninth Armored Division spread all its infantry along the front, separating it from their tanks which were located further back.

General Monteuffel further discovered that the American

First Army patrolled all roads and trails during daylight hours and had the front well defended in most places, but at dark all patrol activities ceased and all front line troops were pulled back to small villages and towns to eat, and sleep. Before daylight next day, they all returned to the front. This practice left only a few isolated outposts on duty where they could possibly see or hear anything of German maneuvers.

The German High Command had ordered a massive artillery barrage just prior to its assault. But Monteuffel cancelled this plan saying, "Why wake them up? They're already asleep". Instead, he ordered the TwentySixth V.G. Infantry Division to infiltrate American positions and surround villages containing companies and battalions. This strategy began about 0200 hours on 16 December. By 0530 hours the German Infantry had crossed the Our River and several small streams to the east and were poised for their attack. When the Americans went to chow at that time, they discovered the Germans and began to fight them.

The German Infantry attacked with force and with intense artillery fire. Also by this time the Germans had put in bridges over the Our and several small streams and pushed the Second Panzer and Panzer-Lear Divisions into the now expanding bridge head.

The stage was now set while our Division was in the Saar-Moselle triangle engaged in heavy fighting to breach the switch position of the Siegfried Line between those two unfordable Saar and Moselle Rivers and located generally about fifteen to twenty miles south of Trier. We had Infantry Divisions on our right and left. The ideas was to break through their fortified position consisting of tank traps, mine fields, and pill boxes to clear out the entire triangle of German troops. Action was interrupted when an urgent coded message was received from XX Corp Headquarters ordering General Morris to meet with Corp and Third Army Commanding Generals in Thionville at 1630 hours on 17 December. General Morris took with him the G-2, G-3, a Division Engineer Officer and myself. We had the only set of maps of the area of Luxembourg and Bastogne available to any of the commanders at that meeting. It was the policy of our Division Engineers to send out officers to the Corps and armies on each flank of the position we were to occupy when our Division was first ordered into a new area. This was because our Division moved quickly and fought over great distances. No one knew when an order from Corp or Army would send us off in a new direction perhaps to execute a fast breakthrough and end run so it was imperative to have maps of all adjacent areas as well. Based on these Tenth Division maps, the battle order sending us to Bastogne was formulated.

The three principal generals were Patton, Walker, and Morris. General Patton explained the situation this way: The Germans had launched a huge attack along the front which included the First Army area to our north and Luxembourg in the Third Army's area. This attack began 16 December and included masses of tanks with the usual large infantry and artillery forces.

Third Army Headquarters had just been moved to Luxembourg City. The entire country of Luxembourg was supposed to have been a quiet front and so the Fourth Infantry Division had been assigned to man its borders even though it was only at fifty percent strength due to recently having been through heavy fighting in the Hurtgen Forest. Being exhausted and at half-strength, they were given this "quiet" front to defend. Their defense strategy consisted of strong points connected by jeep patrol over the entire forty mile long front. Visibility was very limited in this area due to the vaulted structure of the terrain and its heavily wooded areas. These vaults extended through eastern Luxembourg and southern Belgium and areas south of Trier along the Saar River system. This is one of the few areas on earth where faults run at right angles to the existing river lines. The Fourth Infantry Division and the country of Luxembourg were under Third Army Command.

The First Army - Third Army boundary ran roughly east and west at the northern edge of Luxembourg and the southern edge of Belgium. North of this line, Patton had no authority but was told by Eisenhower to turn his army north and drive into the left flank of Von Rundstedt's thrust.

Patton ordered Morris to pull his Tenth Armored Division out of the line under cover of darkness and a heavy artillery barrage that night and and move seventy-five miles north through Luxembourg City into the Luxembourg area and its surrounding road network. First, he was to stop the German drive and then force a wedge into Von Rundstedt's flank.

Further, General Morris was to be "Provisional Corp Commander" of the Fourth Infantry Division and other Third Army troops. He also was to disregard the old First - Third Army boundaries and persuade any troops in the First Army area to cooperate with him in the assault north of the Duchy of

Luxembourg. Notice the words "cooperate and persuade". The Provisional status as Corp Commander was to be General Morris until such time as General Eddy could move and redirect his XII Corp to take over from General Morris.

Further, on the Belgium front, just north of Luxembourg, a "green" Combat Command R of the Ninth Armored Division had been placed recently under the First Army "to settle it down" on this quiet front before sending it into anticipated later action. After some forty years, if my memory serves me correctly, the Combat Command R of the Ninth Armored Division separated their infantry units, putting them in line in their front while positioning their Armored Units on high ground to the rear and some distance in back of the Infantry. Remembering that these troops were green and had never seen an enemy before, one can readily understand what happened when Von Rundstedt suddenly and unexpectedly lunged at them in a major attack. The Germans quickly separated the armor and infantry and chopped them up piecemeal. Many of the Ninth were killed or wounded and many threw aside their guns and fled in panic. A few small units did fight and fell back in proper fashion joining elements of our Division where they gave an excellent account of themselves. The entire Combat Command R of the Ninth Armored Division lasted about two days and never again was a viable unit of that Division until it was later reconstituted with fresh troops and equipment.

In the meantime, General Morris returned to our Division's Headquarters where he held a meeting with all senior commanders and explained the plan to pull out of the Saar-Moselle Triangle under cover of darkness while the adjacent infantry divisions were to "slide sideways" and cover our silent departure; radio silence was in effect. Combat Command B was to lead, then Combat Command A, Combat Command R and then Division rear units would follow. No lights were allowed. The march was to be over secondary roads generally to our west and then we would turn north on the main Thionville-Luxembourg-Bastogne Highway which would lead us directly into the German flank.

Thus our Tenth Armored Division moved all night through darkness, fog, and snow showers over the slippery, crowned black-top roads to Eastern Luxembourg to shore up the Fourth Infantry Division clearing out enemy troops infiltrating down the faults into Luxembourg. Our Combat Command B was held in reserve, however.

Lieutenant Bunt led the heavy engineer equipment from our Switch Position northward to Luxembourg. The road was crowned and slippery as well as difficult to see due to storm and fog. The heavy earth-moving equipment was so hard to keep out of the ditches that he ordered his men to use their headlights, a violation of orders from Division but there was no other way that his drivers could control those large tractor-trailers with their top heavy loads. They arrived safely in the designated area before daylight that morning.

The Germans were sending three Infantry Division which included a mountain division on skis through these faults. For the next seven days and nights, our Combat Command A and Combat Command R attacked enemy troops and cleared these areas. The enemy troops were coming through these draws or faults as their only feasible route to infiltrate Luxembourg City and blow up highway and railroad bridges south of town. This action would prevent Patton's troops from attacking the southern or left flank of Von Rundstedt's Panzer Armies.

On Monday, 18 December, our Combat Command B was rushed to defend Bastogne. The Eighth Corp Commander, General Middleton, ordered the Combat Command B to locate each of its three Task Forces as follows: On the Ettlebruck-Bastogne Highway, in Longvilly to the east, and in Noville to the north. This misguided order was wrong on four critical counts. First, the Senior Commander had no right to designate the exact defensive location of the lower units unless he and or its subordinate commander had made a joint personal inspection of the terrain as to its feasibility for defense or unless the subordinate commander recommended the location of his units after his hands-on inspection of the terrain. Second, each of these task forces was on roads that radiated out like spokes of a wheel from Bastogne, and furthermore they were so far apart they could not support each other militarily. Third, they were so far from our artillery position at Bastogne, that our artillery could fire only about four hundred yards behind enemy lines. Ideally, an artillery in a defensive position should be able to reach two thousand yards behind enemy lines. Fourth, our Combat Command B had no reserve troops at Bastogne.

How could such an inconceivable order be given by such a competent general? The clue is found in the word "panic". Middleton and his staff had been two days and two nights on roads and trails trying to stop troops from retreating and turn them around to fight once again.

As soon as he had set up a "front or stop", he would move

on to the next spot and repeat this strategy. However, as the first shell arrived from the advancing German Army these "stops or fronts" would dissolve and American troops would panic and flee once more. You would not hear this from professionals, but the First Army was in route! General Middleton even moved his headquarters from Bastogne before noon on 18 December back to the west to a safer town.

Task Force O'Hara was assigned defensive positions on the Bastogne-Ettlebruck road, and arrived before nightfall. Inspecting the terrain, O'Hara immediately set up a strong defense as a major attack was imminent. This Bastogne-Ettlebruck road was the only high speed road to Bastogne. Task Force Cherry drew the most difficult assignment as his unit moved due east directly into the teeth of the German advance. Colonel Cherry moved out ahead of his Task Force to inspect the situation at Longvilly. Cherry's teams were Team Hyduk and Team Ryerson which followed in trace.

Colonel Cherry arrived at Longvilly after dark, about 1900 hours, to find this little village occupied by Headquarters Combat Command R of the Ninth Armored Division with all roads out of it blocked by their vehicles. They were in complete turmoil as all of their three Task Forces had been overrun and destroyed by the Germans. Heavy gun flashes lit the eastern sky and the distant roar of explosions was prelude to the approaching fire storm. Colonel Gilbreath, Combat Command R Commander, assured Colonel Cherry that they could hold the town.

Colonel Cherry realized that he could not possible carry out his orders to defend Longvillly due to the presence of

Combat Command R of the Ninth Armored Division. Because it was night time, Cherry did not know that Longvilly was situated in a bowl with a ridge of high ground all around it. The road from Magaret to Longvilly was narrow, twisted, and wound through dense forests. Often along both sides of this road were religious shrines that further impeded deployment off the road. Cherry ordered Hyduk off the road near Longvilly while Ryerson was forced to deploy on the wooded road. Cherry then drove back to Bastogne to explain to Colonel W. Roberts what was happening and requested his orders be clarified. Roberts was totally unaware of the desperate situation at Longvilly.

Task Force Desobry arrived in Bastogne on his way to Noville after dark. The situation at his designated defense position was unclear. He sent two reconnaissance platoons out ahead of his main force to assess the situation. They found the town deserted, or so they thought! Hence, Task Force Desobry moved into Noville. The rest of the night was uneventful except for straggling solders coming back through our lines. One infantry platoon, intact with vehicles, arrived from the Combat Command R Ninth Armored Division and asked it it could stay and fight with Desobry's Task Force. These men were so angry and chagrined at their own Combat Command R's not standing and fighting, they fought beside us like tigers. By midnight Desobry's defense was established. Lieutenant Bill Hanel of "C" Company of the Fifty Fifth Engineers was seriously wounded in his back by shrapnel and was evacuated to England at this time.

While our Combat Command B Tenth Armored Division was deploying east, north, and south to Bastogne on 18 December, the One Hundred First Airborne Division was billeted near Paris, one hundred miles west. Its members were hastily loaded onto trucks and ordered to go immediately to Bastogne but not told why. It was shipped out so fast many of its officers arrived in dress uniform and some men had neither ammunition, weapons, nor winter boots. The lead element of the One Hundred First arrived just after midnight the 19 December. All being quiet in Bastogne, they sacked out in railroad warehouses and in a school building in the south west corner of town. Next morning, our Headquarters Combat Command B and our Four Hundred Twenty Armored Field Artillery Battalion furnished them with everything they were lacking.

Few people know the story of the meeting of Brigadier General McAuliffe and our Combat Command B Colonel Roberts. Roberts was an astute tactician who was retained by the Army at the Command and Staff College to instruct field grade and higher officers of the Army, Navy and Marine Corp. He was so competent that he actually was held back and never did receive adequate opportunities for promotions. He taught Generals Eisenhower, Patton, Bradley, McAuliffe and others. When they met again, the student Brigadier General McAuliffe out-ranked his beloved and respected teacher, Colonel Roberts. There is a policy in the Army that the senior ranking officer present at any station is in command of all units in that area. Nevertheless, their meeting was extremely cordial; whereupon McAuliffe asked Roberts to suggest what he, McAuliffe, should do.

I can almost hear this unflappable, scholarly, and fatherly Colonel say to his former student:

"Well Mac, it's really quite simple. Make all your cooks and drivers infantrymen. Then take those few one hundred five mm. artillery rounds you brought and give them to our Four Hundred Twentieth Armored Field Artillery Battalion. As you know your howitzer tubes are circumcised twenty seven inches and can only fire five thousand yards, but the same ammo in our full length howitzers can fire twelve thousand three hundred yards. Make your artillery men infantry too. In the last two days our S-2 section has identified five infantry divisions and two Panzer divisions in our area. This translates to over ninety thousand enemy as opposed to sixty two hundred men in our Combat Command B plus nine thousand men in your little division. (A regular infantry division is eighteen thousand three hundred men.) With this disparity in numbers, the enemy will try to attack and drive us out, but if it can't, then it will slowly encircle us. So make a "doughnut" around the Bastogne area as fast as possible and then we will pull the armored infantry and tanks back to the center of the doughnut and when an attack is signaled by you, we will send out the fire brigade and put out the fire." And this is exactly what McAuliffe did!

In the meantime about twelve km. east and south of Bastogne the "pot was boiling". General Boyerlein and his Panzer-Lear Division was advancing through broken resistance of the Twenty Eighth Infantry and Ninth Armored Division Combat Command R toward Bastogne on the Wiltz-Ettlebruck-Bastogne road. The Twenty Eighth fought a fierce, delaying action and held up the German's attack on 16 through 18 December. Bayerlein split his forces into two groups at Ettlebruck to take advantage of a road net. The advance guard took the left road and Bayerlein took the right with most of his tanks and all his Infantry Grenadier Regiment.

At the tiny village of Niederwanpack, Bayerlein saw a road leading off which was not on his map but seemed to be pointed directly toward Bastogne. The General stopped his column and asked a farmer if this was a good road. The farmer said it was. What the farmer meant was that it was a good farm market road. But the General assumed he meant it was a good secondary road capable of supporting heavy armor, so Bayerlein proceeded on this road. One must remember that it was about 2400 hours and dark with considerable fog. All Bayerlein could actually see was a snow-filled track in the five inch deep snow where a vehicle had traveled the preceding night.

This road wound down hill and after about three miles it dead-ended in a farmer's barnyard, so it went nowhere! Besides, this entire lower area was underlaid with spongy subsoil. Heavy tanks badly damaged this road, resulting in the entire column "bellying down" in mud. The next few hours his troops spent winching free vehicles so as to get back upon higher and firmer ground. About this time, a report reached Bayerlein that an armored division with a Major General in command had traveled the road to Longvilly after dark the previous evening. The only unit that could possible be taken for an armored division going to Longvilly was Colonel Cherry's forty tanks and forty six half-tracks carrying infantry. This news scared the hell out of Bayerlein, as it would put a large, powerful American unit on his flank. After freeing the tanks and assault guns, he ordered some of them north to the ridge overlooking Longvilly to protect his flanks. One tank company was sent to Magaret and

Refer to maps on pages 268 & 269.

chased Colonel Cherry's Headquarters and Headquarters Company out, then fortified the village. Then Colonel Cherry, returning to Bastogne, ran into a German road block at Magaret and discovered that his Headquarters had moved about two miles south to Neffe Chateau. Cherry also found that adjacent to Neffe Chateau was a railroad siding and shed called Neffe Station which was defended by one platoon of the One Hundred Fifty Eighth Army Engineers. The Engineer Platoon leader, without being told, had set out a tank mine field in front of Neffe Station and a defense to cover it with machine guns, mortars and small arm's fire, a standard procedure.

Just before daylight, General Bayerlein decided to send his Panzer Infantry Regiment on foot between Neffe Chateau and Neffe Station as one of his patrols had incorrectly radioed him that those two locations were now in German hands, but they were not! Due to darkness and heavy fog which prevented men from seeing more than ten feet, the Panzer Infantry Regiment Commander, to keep control, formed his men in close order columns of three abreast with one company closed up behind the one ahead. Walking over open fields, they headed for Bastogne between Neffe Chateau and Neffe Station.

Shortly after daybreak, this enemy regiment began passing between Neffe Chateau and Neffe Station when suddenly the fog lifted.

Troops who were there said to their utter astonishment they observed a massed enemy regiment directly in front of their machine guns. The resulting cross-fire from Colonel Cherry's Task Force and the Engineer Platoon and help from our Four Hundred Twentieth Field Artillery Battalion at Bastogne and the newly arrived Five Hundred First Regiment of One Hundred First Airborne Division destroyed the German regiment. This was the third time in a relatively short period that the Panzer-Lear Division had lost all its infantry.

Bayerlein had stopped his main tank force, holding it back, waiting for the expected main American attack against his right flank by the Armored Division which had been incorrectly reported in the area of Longvilly. It was here that General Monteuffel found him waiting. This Fifth Panzer Army Commander "blew his top" and all five foot one inch of him soared three feet off the ground and shouted, "You fool! You violated your orders to go directly to Bastogne and take it!" But Bayerlein was more worried about the reported Armored Division on his flank.

Bayerlein was a Bavarian and Monteuffel a Prussian. Within the German Officer Corp Bavarians thought Prussians were "stuffed shirts" and the Prussians believed Bavarians were "hicks".

This fear of Bayerlein had been incited early that morning by the terrific attack that our Captain Hyduk had launched to attempt to take the ridge south of Longvilly and the attack which Captain Ryerson's troops had made against Magaret trying to break out of its entrapment. These actions had been ordered by Colonel Cherry. By early afternoon, Hyduk had again attacked the south ridge attempting to dislodge German tanks; again he failed.

Unknown to our men at Longvilly, the Second Panzer Division had proceeded before daylight that morning north toward Bursey and Noville. Enroute they dropped off their eighty-eight assault guns on the north ridge overlooking Longvilly, to protect their flanks. They knew something was there but not what! Hyduk's first attack failed not only due to Panzer-Lear tanks and assault guns on the south ridge and their Division's artillery fire, but also the Second Panzer Division's eighty-eights shooting them in their backsides. With all the firing, no one realized what was really occurring at the time.

The second attack by Hyduk in the early afternoon failed not only because of these enemy actions, but also because the Twenty-Sixth Volks-Grenadier Division began to attack his troops and Longvilly from the east. It was then Hyduk realized that the eighty-eights had been shooting him in the back in <u>both</u> operations.

At daylight the morning of 20 December, the Twenty Sixth Volks-Grenadier Infantry Division was so tired from three days and nights of constant marching on foot to keep up with two Panzer tank divisions plus fighting our Twenty Eighth Infantry Division and Combat Command R of Ninth Armored Division that it went into a wooded area east of Longvilly to rest and sleep. The fact that the Twenty Sixth V.G. Division did keep up with their tanks was an outstanding feat.

During the morning hours of 20 December, 1944, the German Corp Commander, General Luttwitz, lost track of his Twenty Sixth Volks-Grenadier Infantry Division. He went looking for it and to his chagrin located it asleep in a forest about noon. He ordered it to attack Longvilly immediately, and so their attack was launched about 1400 hours that afternoon. At this hour, Captain Hyduk's second attack against tanks on the south ridge was in full swing. It was rough for one Armored

Infantry Company, now reduced by its previous losses, to withstand the fire of two enemy division's artillery, one infantry regiment, tanks, and eighty-eights assault guns firing from all sides.

At this junction, Hyduk had only two tanks and three half-tracks remaining of twenty tanks and twenty-three half-tracks, so he withdrew to the road and around the corner into the protection of the woods. He was at least out of direct fire from tanks on the south ridge and eighty-eights on the north ridge. His forward artillery observer called for a Time-on-Target barrage on the infantry regiment attacking over open fields from east to west toward Longvilly. This Time-on-Target fired by the Four Hundred Twentieth Armored Field Artillery Battalion, practically destroyed the lead enemy infantry regiment.

Results of this Time-on-Target were to disrupt the Twenty Sixth V.G. Infantry attack. It had to fall back and re-group before re-attacking. Darkness had now settled in. Unknown to either the Twenty Sixth V.G. Infantry Division and the Panzer-Lear Division, the Second Panzer Division had pulled their eighty-eights from the north ridge in early afternoon as they needed them further north at Noville. Also, one regiment of the Twenty Sixth began to move north along the Longvilly ridge and the valley beyond, towards Noville.

At the launching of the German Twenty Sixth V.G. Infantry Division's attack that afternoon at Longvilly, all the Combat Command R of the Ninth Armored Division panicked and piled into its vehicles and headed toward Magaret. The tanks on the south ridge and eighty-eights on the north ridge opened fire on this exodus. Now Task Force Hyduk had even greater difficulty maneuvering due to burning and exploding Ninth Armored Division vehicles on the road.

Hyduk and Ryerson radioed Colonel Cherry that they could not <u>bust</u> the Germans and that they had lost many men and much armor. Cherry advised them to withdraw or infiltrate any way they could, to Neffe Chateau after dark.

Hyduk fired all of his tank ammo at the enemy and at dusk destroyed his two remaining tanks plus the three half-tracks. Every able bodied man and officer remaining in his unit then shouldered upwards of two hundred pounds each of extra ammo and machine guns or carried a wounded man piggy-back. This group in single file followed a compass course and started through the forest toward Neffe Chateau. One can only imagine the great physical difficulty of this trek. Stumbling along in the dark and snow, the men skinned their shins on rocks and dead-falls, tripped up repeatedly on tree roots and rocks hidden beneath the snow or stepped unwittingly into holes waist deep. After four hours of this exhausting effort, they arrived safely at Neffe Chateau where the wounded were immediately evacuated to the field hospital at Bastogne. The rest physically and psychologically exhausted collapsed onto the hard stone floor of that chateau.

Captain Ryerson had a different situation; he had located a foot path through the forest which led directly to Neffe Chateau. His problem was that this foot path was too narrow for tanks and half-tracks! To solve this predicament, he sent all of his infantry forward with axes and saws, chopping down all trees over five inches in diameter for a distance of five feet on either side of this path. Next, he sent his tanks forward and these thirty-three ton brutes pushed over all smaller trees and brush; their steel treads chewed up stumps and limbs. Next went his remaining half-tracks and their treads helped also. At the end of the procession, came a couple of two-and-a-half ton ammo trucks and two jeeps. They all arrived at Neffe Chateau about the same time as Captain Hyduk's men. Colonel Cherry's Task Force was once again together even though badly depleted.

Colonel Cherry met with Colonel Julian Ewell, the Five Hundred First Regiment Commander of the One Hundred First Division and planned a joint attack on Magaret for daylight 21 December.

Before daylight the morning of the 20th, in other words some eighteen hours earlier, General McAuliffe had met with Colonel Roberts and then issued an incredible order to Colonel Julian Ewell to proceed down the Longvilly road and take Wiltz. The One Hundred First Airborne Division did not know who or what was at Magaret or what was going on. Colonel Ewell was so astute he had no intention of going to Wiltz as it was already twenty miles behind German lines! As he could hear all the firing ahead, he dismounted his men just outside of Bastogne and formed an approach march. It was dark and foggy, hence his visibility was limited to ten feet. He placed himself on the Bastogne-Magaret-Longvilly road with one Battalion of Infantry on his left and one Battalion on his right. The Third Battalion followed him in squad columns. Out in front he sent a point which consisted of an officer and a radio operator. Colonel Ewell had radio communications with each of his Battalion Commanders as well as with the "point". Two of his Battalions were abreast of him and with each man no more than eight feet apart in order to see his neighbor. This approach formation moved about one quarter mile per hour through the snow and fog feeling their way forward. Just before daylight his right Battalion came upon our Neffe Chateau and Neffe Station defenses, so Colonel Ewell immediately ordered his men to take defensive positions. When the fog lifted, some of their machine guns helped destroy the Panzer-Lear Grenadier Infantry Regiment mentioned previously. All that day they backed up Colonel Cherry's men and the One Hundred Fifty Eighth Engineers Platoon at Neffe Station. Skirmishes and battle raged along this front.

Colonel Jim O'Hara's Task Force sat astride the Ettlebruck-Bastogne road expecting momentary attack. But because General Bayerlein had turned north off the road, this section was quiet.

On the night of the 19-20th, Major Bill Desobry's Task Force had left Bastogne and proceeded up to Noville under cover of darkness; all was quiet until early morning of the 20th.

By then, the Second Panzer Division had turned north from the Longvilly road and on to Bourcy heading toward Noville. Before daylight, one of Desobry's outposts challenged some tanks and infantry trying to pass them. They were a forward platoon of the Second Panzer Division and answered the challenge with fire. Whereupon our men showered them with tank fire and grenades thus driving them off and alerting us to their presence. Their German platoon leader reported to Colonel Lauchert that our defenses were too strong to overcome. At this point Major Desobry ordered this outpost back to our main lines of defense in Noville. Shortly thereafter, he ordered the other two outposts back also because he could hear through the fog, enemy troops and tanks moving about on the east, north, and northwest of our positions. When the fog finally cleared about 1000 hours, our men could see arrayed before them the entire Second Panzer Division. They were looking down on Noville from a ridge that stretches one third of the way around Noville - east, north, and northwest. German artillery and eighty-eights began pounding us in Noville. After a fierce preparation, their tanks and infantry came out of the hills toward Noville, and so we opened up with everything we had. A Battalion of forty tanks led the assault; this initial attack lasted two hours. During that time, our gunners destroyed thirty two Panzer tanks and nearly wiped out one infantry regiment. Their losses were eight hundred killed and over eight hundred wounded. This action was a wild affair. During the height of the battle, one of their Mark IV tanks penetrated our defenses and pushed to the center of town. Here it was subjected to so much thirty and fifty caliber machine gun fire and thirty seven and forty mm. fire its tank crew panicked and fled leaving its engine idling and its radio blaring. So much for claustrophobia!

So far, Major Desobry's losses[2] had been two hundred killed and over one hundred twenty wounded. Also, we lost eleven tanks and four half-tracks. The northern edge of town was reduced to rubble, and other parts were in flames. Major Bill Desobry radioed Colonel Roberts that he wished to withdraw to a ridge line at Foy where his troops would have better terrain to defend. Colonel Roberts responded by asking him to stay there as he was sending Colonel LaPrade with the Glider Battalion of the One Hundred First to help. Desobry

---

[2] Data from Lieutenant General Desobry's tape.

agreed to stay. The Glider Battalion arrived about 1200 hours and both Commanders agreed to attack the north and east ridges at 1400 hours. With a five minute smoke preparation and barrage by our Four Hundred Twentieth Armored Field Artillery Battalion at Bastogne, our armored infantry and tanks headed up the various roads and the Glider Battalion attacked between them.

Would you believe the Second Panzer Division decided to attack us at the exact same time! They came out of the hills and we in turn came out of the town!

All elements of the Second Panzer Division attacked, including the eighty-eights they had pulled from the north ridge overlooking Longvilly, so no one got anywhere. One company of the Glider Battalion pushed half way to the top of the ridge and were thrown back with great losses; another made it to the ridge and was driven back. Before dark, all our troops were pulled back into Noville and the Second Panzer Division pulled back into the hills. This time, Colonel Roberts agreed to let Desobry's men pull back to Foy and the ridge line.

Major Desobry and Colonel LaPrade met in a stone building in Noville to plan their withdrawal back to Foy. A radio equipped half-track happened to pull up to this building. A German tank fired at it and missed but hit the building killing Colonel LaPadre instantly and wounding Major Desobry, who was carried off unconscious. Major Hustead immediately took command of Desobry's Task Force. At this time, one regiment of the Twenty Sixth V.G. Infantry Division attacked between Noville and Foy. Noville defenders were now surrounded. A blazing tank infantry attack south to Foy ensued. Our forces ripped a great hole in the Twenty Sixth and so arrived safely at Foy after intense fighting.

This last day, 21 December, the road was open enabling General Morris and me to go to Bastogne where he conferred with General McAuliffe and Colonel Roberts. Morris was still the Provisional Corp Commander as well as Commanding General of the Tenth Armored Division. The General kept fretting about rumors of the Germans trying to cut the road south and, as he had many "irons in the fire" in many areas, he finished his business as quickly as possible. About a mile outside Bastogne on that snow covered road, our jeep ran out of gas. Quickly the General hopped out of the right front seat and held it up so I could pour gas into the tank from our spare five gallon can. Thereupon he ordered our driver to start up and move out as fast as possible, so fast in fact yours truly hardly had time to grab the rear base of the machine gun mount and crawl in over the jeep's rear gate while still holding the partially empty spare gas tank with my other hand. We had not traveled over two hundred yards on this snow covered road, when out of the forest, came the lead platoon of German troops at the exact spot where we had refueled. Their leader fired a burp gun at us but missed us by an inch or so as our jeep had picked up speed to about forty miles an hour and the road curved downhill to the right. Obviously this Kraut never heard of "Kentucky windage" for which I was profoundly grateful. One can imagine what would have happened had his gun's steel jacketed bullets hit the partially full gas can I still held in my hand.

During the afternoon of 20 December, 1944, a German patrol picked up the Mayor of Bastogne. He was immediately hauled before the Fifth Panzer Army Commander, General Monteuffel. He asked him how much American armor was in the Bastogne area. Since the honorable Mayor wanted the U.S. to win, he looked the German Commander directly in the eye and lied to him by stating there were ten Armored Divisions in Bastogne!

Miracle of miracles, the General believed him partly due to the sudden and total loss of all the Panzer-Lear Infantry Regiment, three other regiments and the three terrific attacks by Colonel Cherry's men near Longvilly and Major Desobry's two attacks at Noville.

From this point on General Monteuffel became very, very cautious. After Bastogne was encircled at 1100 hours on the 21st, he would launch an attack in one sector. Our "Fire Brigade" attack would go out and drive the enemy back. Then General Monteuffel would try in another sector. Once again our "Fire Brigade" did its job. It never occurred to the Germans to attack in two areas simultaneously. If they had, Bastogne would have fallen like a paper house as we had only enough tanks and armored infantry to handle one attack at a time.

I salute the good and faithful men and officers of our elite Tenth Armored Division. As one who was among you those terrible days and nights seemingly without end, I salute you for great courage, extreme humility, enormous love of freedom and stern self-discipline. Truly, there were no heroes - just ordinary men doing extraordinary things - but brothers all.

ENEMY PARATROOPS

One event of interest took place just prior to the afternoon of 15 December. A Colonel Vanderhedt, who was a German Parachute Commander, had orders to drop his troops on the evening of that day, just after dark, in northern Belgium near the First U.S. Army Headquarters at Spa. His five hundred paratroopers had been situated in a holding area near Frankfort, Germany, and trucks were to pick them up at dusk and deliver them to an airfield. New, more powerful radios had been given them. However, the trucks never arrived so Colonel Vanderhedt phoned General Seth Dietrick who was the Sixth Panzer S.S. Army Commander to inform him that he needed trucks to transport his men and their new radios to the airfield. General Dietrick told him to find his own G—D— trucks! Vanderhedt was asked why his Commanding General would respond this way. His reply was that Dietrick was an alcoholic and he was always drunk, even that night. So the next day, Vanderhedt found some trucks and this delayed his drop until the evening of 16 December.

Due to pilot errors, darkness and heavy overcast, this five hundred man force was scattered all the way from the Rhine River to Northern Belgium — in other words, they were lost! Only about thirty troops landed near Spa and they were ten miles north of the city entirely off Vanderhedt's maps. It took Vanderhedt a whole day to figure out exactly where he was. As no German paratroops had been dropped since the battle for Crete early in the war, they had forgotten how to pack their radios properly and all their new radios were destroyed on landing.

The Germans discovered that Americans patrolled roads during the day, but after dark holed up in villages and towns. So Vanderhedt and his men moved about freely after dark and waylaid anything coming through. Also the First Army had a very poor practice of sending out couriers to all units by jeep and motorcycle every morning at exactly 0800 hours with complete orders for all units and maps for the day.

Each morning, the Germans would capture one or two couriers and so had complete orders for the entire First Army. They were totally frustrated because their new radios did not function and so they could not relay information to the German High Command. After a few days, they realized that they were absolutely ineffective and so decided to work their way back by night to their German lines. The group that Colonel Vanderhedt commanded stumbled into the Ninety Ninth Infantry Division and were all captured.

POTATOES

There are two more singular human events of interest: The first one concerned the village of Noville. When Major Desobry first arrived at Noville, he and his men searched it completely. It was deserted - or so they thought. Actually, the town's schoolmaster and his ten-year old son and three other men had hidden themselves by burrowing deep beneath a large pile of potatoes in the cellar of the schoolhouse. At the time our men never knew they were there, since these five stayed out of sight until after the Americans had left and the firing ceased. Supposing all troops, both U.S. and German, were gone, the little group came out of hiding to see what had happened to their village. The Germans saw them and thinking they were left by the Americans to spy on the Nazis, they promptly marched them to the rear of the village church where his son was forced to watch his father and the other men executed.

FIFTH COLUMN

One of the other concerns we all had was the local activities of the German Fifth Column Unit under Colonel Stranzani. This Nazi officer was a past master at counter-intelligence. Long before 1939, the Nazis had trained and placed in every country of Europe men and women who were Quisling's to their own country. In all cases, these local citizens were trained in two-way radio operations, map reading, observation techniques of defense installations and supply dumps, enemy morale, and other pertinent skills of value to the German High Command. Naturally our Division was concerned about the possibility of threat from this underground. Actually, little or no such activities took place in our area of the Ardennes at the Battle of the Bulge. Some action of this nature did take place earlier during our battles across France and Belgium. To my knowledge the Germans employed much more direct means than this Corp during this period, such as: Colonel Vanderhedt's Airborne drop, previously noted, and the Marquis' troops.

THE MARQUIS

The Marquis was a relative of the King of Belgium and as such, the Allies considered him a reliable friend; actually, he was just another Quisling. After World War I, the Treaty of Versailles annexed a ten mile wide strip of German ground to

Belgium, which then became the eastern side of Belgium. The idea was that it was to be a buffer against any future German war efforts. The population of this strip remained loyal Germans, spoke the language and retained German customs, and remained loyal to the Fatherland. The Marquis recruited his followers from these Germans even though they were legally citizens of Belgium. We equipped them to guard bridges, supply dumps, et al behind our lines.

Actually, they scouted ahead of Von Rundstedt's Armies reporting to it all our deployed locations and artillery positions. This group "captured" our field hospital near Bastogne and turned it over to the German Army. This is how Major Bill Desobry[3] (now Lt. General) was captured while he lay wounded in that hospital.

The Marquis Group stole a few of Combat Command R Ninth Division's half-tracks and attempted to disrupt our defenses by pretending to be retreating U.S. troops. This scheme didn't work because when they were challenged none of them could answer which league the Detroit Tigers baseball team belonged to. They may have had our passwords and counter signs, but they didn't know American baseball!

---

[3] Please refer to the two maps at the end of this book.

ORGANIZATION OF C.C.B. TENTH ARMORED DIVISION HEADQUARTERS C.C.B.

Medical & Dental Unit

Signal Platoon

Engineer Company

420th Armored Field Arty. Bn.

Military Police Platoon

Reconnaisance Troop "D"

"C" Co. 21st Tank Bn.

Col. O'Hara   (Task Force) equal number tanks & infantry

Col. Cherry   (Task Force) equal number tanks & infantry

Maj. Desobry (Task Force) equal number tanks & infantry

Attached Tank Destroyer Co.

Ninth Air Force Forward Controller

Attached Mobile Anti-Aircraft Co.

Maintenance Platoon (Motor)

Ordinance Platoon (Small Arms)

Support Units not attached to C.C.B.

Army Field Hospital

Truck Supply Company

6500 Enlisted Men and Officers

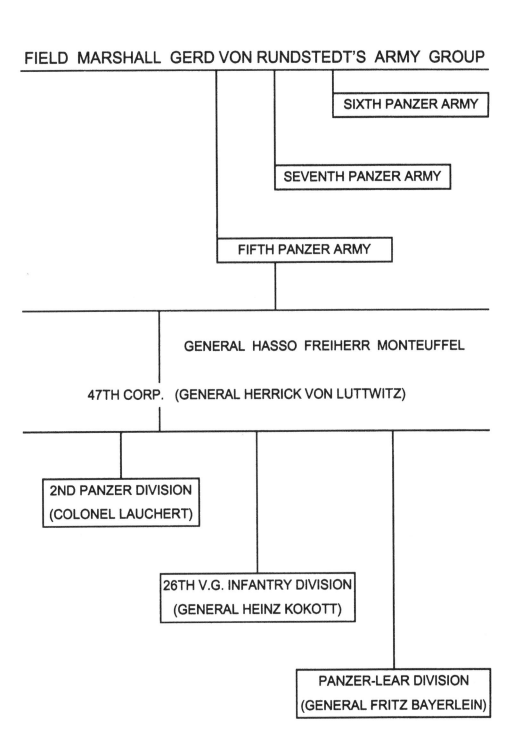

FIELD MARSHALL GERD VON RUNDSTEDT'S ARMY GROUP

SIXTH PANZER ARMY

SEVENTH PANZER ARMY

FIFTH PANZER ARMY

GENERAL HASSO FREIHERR MONTEUFFEL

47TH CORP.   (GENERAL HERRICK VON LUTTWITZ)

2ND PANZER DIVISION
(COLONEL LAUCHERT)

26TH V.G. INFANTRY DIVISION
(GENERAL HEINZ KOKOTT)

PANZER-LEAR DIVISION
(GENERAL FRITZ BAYERLEIN)

13
Patton's Prayer

Prayer given before dawn 23 December 1944 for clear weather.

"Almighty and most merciful Father, we humbly beseech Thee, of Thy great goodness, to restrain these immoderate rains with which we have had to contend. Grant us fair weather for Battle. Graciously hearken to us as soldiers who call upon Thee that armed with Thy power, we may advance from Victory, and crush the oppression and wickedness of our enemies, and establish Thy justice among men and nations. Amen."

Note: Immediately after he gave the above prayer, the weather cleared and stayed clear. This prayer had been written by an Army Chaplain who had been pressured into doing it by Patton. When the weather cleared so quickly, Patton declared that anyone having so much influence with God certainly deserved a medal. Patton immediately decorated him.

(Reference: <u>Patton, Ordeal and Triumph</u> by L. Fargo
<u>War as I Knew It</u> by General Patton)

14
Unit Citation

HEADQUARTERS
THIRD UNITED STATES ARMY
APO 403

GENERAL ORDERS   7 February 1945.
NUMBER 31

UNIT CITATION

Under the provisions of Section IV, Circulary 333, War Department, 22 December 1943, the following units are cited:

Combat Command "B", 10th Armored Division, including:
Headquarters and Headquarters Company, Combat Command "B", 10th Armored Division
3d Tank Battalion (Less Company C)
20th Armored Infantry Battalion (Less Company A)
54th Armored Infantry Battalion (Less Companies A and G)
420th Armored Field Artillery Battalion
Troop "D", 90th Cavalry Reconnaissance Squadron (Mechanized)
Company "C", 609th Tank Destroyer Battalion (Less 1st Platoon; with 2d Platoon Reconnaissance Company attached)
Battery "B", 796th Antiaircraft Artillery Automatic Weapons Battalion
Company "C", 55th Armored Engineer Battalion
Company "C", 21st Tank Battalion

These units distinguised themselves in combat against powerful and agressive enemy forces during the period from 18 December to 27 December 1944, by extraordinary heroism and gallantry in defense of the key communications center of BASTOGNE BELGIUM. Essential to a large-scale exploitation of his break-through into BELGIUM and northern LUXEMBOURG, the enemy attempted to seize BASTOGNE by attacking constantly and savagely with the best of his armor and infantry. Without benefit of prepared defenses, facing almost overwhelming odds and with very limited and fast-dwindling supplies, these units maintained a high combat morale and an impenetrable GO

No. 31, Hq Third US Army, 7 Feb 1945, cont'd.

defense, despite extremely heavy bombing, intense artillery fire, and constant attacks from infantry and armor on all side of their completely cut off and encircled position. This masterful and grimly-determined defense denied the enemy even momentary success in an operation for which he paid dearly in men, materiel, and eventually morale. The outstanding courage and resourcefulness and undaunted determination of this gallant force is in keeping with the highest traditions of the service.

By command of Lieutenant General PATTON:

HOBART R. GAY,
Brigadier General, U.S. Army,
Chief of Staff.

HEADQUARTERS VIII CORPS
OFFICE OF THE COMMANDING GENERAL

APO 308, U.S. Army,
17 January 1945.

1st Ind.
HEADQUARTERS 10TH ARMORED DIVISION, U.S. ARMY, APO 260,
23 January 1945.

TO: Officers and Enlisted Men, Combat Command "B" 10th Armored Division.

It gives me great pleasure to forward to you this well-earned letter of commendation.

/s/   W.H.H. Morris, Jr.
W.H.H. MORRIS, JR.,
Major General, United States Army,
Commanding.

HEADQUARTERS
4TH INFANTRY DIVISION
APO 4, US ARMY

SUBJECT: Commendation

AG 201.22 (G-1)   28 December 1944.

1st Ind.
HEADQUARTERS XII CORPS, APO 312, U.S. ARMY, 5 January 1945.

TO: Commanding General, 10th Armored Division, APO 260, U.S. Army.

THRU: Commanding General Third U.S. Army, APO 403, U.S. Army.

It is a pleasure for me to add my own commendation to that of General Blakeley's for the 10th Armored Division's superb performance.

/s/   M.S. Eddy
/t/   M.S. EDDY
Major General, U.S. Army,
Commanding.

AG 201.22 GNMCA-4   28 December 1944.

2d Ind.
HQ THIRD US ARMY, APO 403, U.S. ARMY, 9 January 1945.

THRU: Commanding General, XX Corps, APO 340, U.S. Army.

TO: Commanding General, 10th Armored Division, APO 260, U.S. Army

This well-deserved commendation of the 10th Armored Division for its action during the period cited is forwarded with pleasure and the assurance that these operations will mark a brilliant page in the history of the current campaign.

/s/   G.S. Patton Jr.,
/t/   G.S. PATTON. JR.,
Lieutenant General, U.S. Army,
Commanding.

HEADQUARTERS
4TH INFANTRY DIVISION
APO 4, US ARMY

SUBJECT: Commendation

AG 201.22   28 December 1944.

3d Ind.
HEADQUARTERS XX CORPS, A.P.O. 340, U.S. Army, 13 January 1945.

TO: Commanding General, 10th Armored Division, APO 260, U.S. Army

I have noted the above commendation with a deep feeling of gratification. Such devotion to duty and will to close with the enemy can bring only success on the field of battle. I am proud to have the 10th Armored Division in the XX Corps.

/s/   Walton H. Walker
/t/ WALTON H. WALKER
Major General, United States Army
Commanding

4th Ind.
HEADQUARTERS 10TH ARMORED DIVISION, U.S. ARMY, APO 260,
20 January, 1945.

TO: All Officers and Enlisted Men of the 10th Armored Division.

It is with great pleasure I forward to you this well-earned commendation.

W.H.H. MORRIS, Jr.,
Major General, United States Army,
Commanding.

General Morris decorating
Combat Command "B" with
Unit Citation at Garmish-
Partenkirchen, Germany
May 1945.

15
Siegfried Line

At the conclusion of the Battle of Bastogne, our Division was ordered to return to the normal Third Army front and to attack the German Army on the other side of the Saar River by driving through the Siegfried Line on its eastern bank. The earth here was a geological faulted structure. The axis of the hinged formations or vaults ran east and west while the Saar River ran roughly north and south.

The Germans had fortified the eastern bank of the Saar from the river along the slopes of the faults. Their pill boxes had been expertly built and well camouflaged. Due to the passing of four or five years since they had been built, native vines and shrubs had grown over these pill boxes and their connecting trenches. Thus, observed from a distance, none were visible.

The Ninety Fourth Infantry Division was to attack on the left and our Division on the right, each to gain a bridge-head across the Saar. It must be pointed out that during darkness the night before our assault across the Saar River, the Fifth Ranger Battalion had crossed by stealth. They infiltrated through the Siegfried Line to secure high ground overlooking the road net. The Fifth Ranger Battalion then fired on any vehicles or troops that the German Army tried to bring up. This action disrupted their rear areas. The Germans vigorously attacked these Rangers repeatedly. Although well dug in, these spirited Americans were barely able to hold out until our Tenth Armored troops relieved them. They suffered many casualties and were nearly out of food, water, and ammunition by the time we arrived. Both the Ninety Fourth and our armored infantry made the crossing successfully under cover of darkness, in spite of the river being at flood stage, moving at six miles per hour, and with heavy enemy small arms and artillery fire. Once having a toe hold on the east bank, the Ninety Fourth Infantry and our infantry units consolidated sideways into one enlarged bridge-head.

The Third Army supplied enough materials for two pontoon bridges to be built. The Ninety Fourth put across theirs. Each time our Division's bridge was about to be completed, the enemy destroyed it by artillery fire, so we were never able to complete it.

It was then decided to send our armor and artillery over on the Ninety Fourth's bridge, but then several technical problems immediately arose. First was lack of maneuver room on the east bank for our armored vehicles. Before we could move across the river, our infantry and the Ninety Fourth had to attack further eastward to eliminate some of the enemy's pill boxes and to gain the high ground directly to our collective front, thereby eliminating enemy direct observation and fire on the bridge site.

Second, because of our location on the ground, and our Twentieth Armored Infantry Battalion, Fifty Fourth Armored Infantry Battalion were reversed in relation to their armored personnel carriers. When these personnel carriers crossed the river, these two infantry units wound up in each other's carriers. This would not have ben possible except with a well trained and competent outfit like the Tenth Armored.

One of the techniques we used was to fire our .50 caliber machine guns (better known as wood choppers) across the terrain.   Whenever the stream of tracers made a sudden elevation or change of direction, there was a pill box.   By continuing to fire at that pill box location, the machine guns tore away brush and exposed the exact shape and size of that concrete fortification.   At this point, we either used direct tank or artillery fire to blast these fortifications.   One of the most effective means was to use the 155 mm. gun batteries in direct fire.   When even this measure did not destroy a pill box, it panicked the enemy inside and so they surrendered.

One of the effects of artillery fire upon either tanks or fortifications which most people do not understand is its psychological effect upon its occupants.   With sufficient hammering, men can become "unhinged".   It's the same feeling that the crew members feel after their submarines have dived and then are subject to depth charges.   Only by iron-clad will power and stern discipline can a man survive such panic situations.   Even then, some do "crack".

One of the moments that seemed like an eternity to me was when we crossed a pontoon bridge in an open vehicle while German shells were exploding about eighty feet above our heads.   Our column stopped and we were midstream of the Saar River with all vehicles bumper to bumper and we sat there motionless for about an hour while the fighting continued up ahead.   Fortunately for us, enemy shells never descended or I would not be writing these memoirs now!   My guess was that enemy artillery was in defilade and so thwarted by the high ground ahead that they were unable to lower their bursts to strike at the bridge site.

One of the interesting things during this action concerned a chaplain. He was about 29 years old and right out of seminary. None of the chaplains were required to go further forward than the battalion medical aid stations. Nevertheless this man decided that he should go forward up with our lead infantry platoon in its attack against the pill boxes and trenches. We were using satchel charges on enemy pill boxes. Taking with him only his prayer book, a canteen of water, and some first aid bandages, he crawled forward with our infantry. When one of the men was wounded, he calmed him by quoting the scriptures and bandaging up his wounds until the aid men could safely carry this soldier to the aid station. If a man were dying, he performed last rites and held his hand while reciting the scriptures giving him quiet assurance until he slipped away. When our lads were near panic, his words inspired them, relieving their anxiety. In short, he was a true friend of the staunchest kind. If anyone recalls this chaplain's name, I would be pleased to know it as my memory fails me! He certainly merits our greatest respect.

After breaking through the Siegfried Line, our Division drove to the little mountain road junction of Zerf, and from there turned north to Trier. The narrow mountain road was under direct enemy fire all its distance due to the Krauts being located on high ground on both sides of the road. We dubbed it "The Bowling Alley". It was at Trier that Task Force Richardson captured a bridge intact. You will find this story elsewhere in these writings entitled <u>The Bridge</u>.

16
Zerf, Germany

After we broke through the Siegfried Line about 26 or 27 February, Task Force Richardson was ordered north to make a run to Trier in an attempt to save the three bridges there. General Morris decided to follow Richardson through a mountain pass to Zerf and then north toward Trier. We were in one of the old light tanks commonly referred to as a bucket of bolts. These light tanks were very fast and had good flotation even though their tracks were only seven inches wide. The Germans had the pass and elbow of Zerf under direct observed "88" fire. To run this road was highly dangerous. Our driver was one of the best as he shifted gears rapidly and thus maintained a good speed.

Just as we reached Richardson's tank, a radio message was received in code from our Division Headquarters advising General Morris to return immediately to Division Headquarters as General Patton was on his way there to see him. We immediately started back down the "Bowling Alley".

As our tank rolled downhill on the narrow mountain road to the Zerf corner, we observed a stone house on the right side of the road, a telephone pole on the left and squarely between them blocking the road a burning half-track. Just short of this blockade on our left was a forty foot bank to the main road below that led south and then abruptly turned east back to our Division Headquarters on the other side of the mountain. To the right side of our road was a steep escarpment rising sharply upward 200 feet.

I called the driver on the intercom and told him not to stop but do a hard left over the drop off to the road below, telling the general to hang on as we plunged downward. Our driver quickly down-shifted and turned the tank toward home base as I directed. He shifted gears rapidly and as we moved forward, out of my periscope view, I counted three solid shots that hit the dirt bank on my right. The last round knocked a wooden box full of "C" rations off our tank's rear deck. This was eight inches behind my head — a little too close for comfort to say the least! The only thing that saved us was the speed with which our driver pulled ahead.

Upon reaching our Division Command Post, we met General Patton's jeep as he pulled up. After exchanging salutes and greetings, Patton said that he wanted to see the German horse drawn artillery column that had been caught on the mountain road and destroyed by machine gun fire that morning. General Morris and I looked at each other in dismay. Was that all he wanted? And after all we had come through to be there!

There is some argument about who destroyed this enemy artillery column. As I recall, it was one of our tank units that ran up the back side of this enemy column while others claimed it was the 9th Tactical Air Wing who had machine gunned it. In either case, one of our tank-dosers had run up the column shoving dead men, caissons, horses and guns off the road resulting in a jumbled mess.

Everyone was afraid of Patton and no one at headquarters had been up the road of the destroyed enemy artillery. So after some foot dragging, I volunteered, providing the General would allow me a minute to check the route and location. With my map under one arm, I climbed into the rear seat of Patton's jeep. What a ride! I discovered then why he had air horns on that jeep. Ordinary horns were not loud enough for tank drivers or crews to hear over the noise of the engines and firing. One blast from those air horns moved tanks to one side fast as we sailed past them.

Arriving at the site, Patton got out with his camera and walked the entire length taking photos of the horses which he loved; the dead Krauts he could care less about. Returning to his jeep where his driver and I waited, he said to me, "Lieutenant, take a good look as this is probably the last horse drawn unit you will ever see in any war".

Footnote: To those of us who are interested in field artillery, it should be noted that our War Department changed all artillery from horse drawn to truck or tractor drawn means in 1936. All other armies of the world used exclusively horse drawn artillery through World War II. Even the Panzer Army of General Guderian used horse drawn artillery for the most part. The British had a few truck drawn artillery units also.

One must not confuse the 88's with artillery. Most of these were truck drawn. The Germans considered their 88's as assault guns that could be used also for anti-aircraft fire. Assault guns are used individually and their fires are not massed as we do with artillery.

17
Sergeant T—

One of the few redeeming joys of being in the Armed Forces was knowing some of the finest men and officers of our nation. Fortunately, we had a very large number of them in our Tenth Armored Division; one such person was Sgt. T—.

He was a Tech Sgt. in our One Hundred Fiftieth Signal Company and assigned to Division Headquarters as were several other men to handle the radio traffic including General Morris. The Commanding General's vehicles each had sixteen radio frequency channels which were monitored 24 hours a day as some of these channels were assigned to higher headquarters and adjacent corp and other units. Each day at 1200 hours all of our Division's sixteen channels changed frequencies to keep the enemy confused and "in the dark". They were changed by removing lettered frequency cubes and inserting a new cube into each numbered channel. These cubes were rotated in a random order each day. The frequencies included those for higher headquarters as well as our own Division's units at the tank platoon level. If my memory serves me correctly, each tank or infantry platoon half-track had two or three channels to change at 1200 hours each day. These usually were one frequency for that platoon, one to the company commander, and perhaps one to Battalion optional.

Sometime after Zerf, General Morris handed me an encoded order to be personally delivered to the Task Force

Commander for our attack. It was a hilly area and our Task Force Commander had set up his headquarters in an old stone wood cutter's house beside a deep cut in a hillside road. It was about forty feet deep where the road passed through. I stopped my medium tank in this cut for protection from heavy mortar and artillery fire. Before leaving the tank turret, I instructed Sgt. T— to stay on the radio in the event that I should receive further orders from Division Headquarters or the General; this he did. I no sooner climbed out of the tank than the enemy spotted it and began to fire salvos from a battery of four One Hundred Twenty mm. mortars. The enemy obviously had zeroed this cut in. One Hundred Twenty mm. mortars are six inch shells which translate to medium artillery. One or more of these shells falling upon a heavy tank could destroy or badly damage it. It just so happened that these Nazi gunners had set our exact elevation on their mortar sights, so their artillery should have hit our tank on the first salvo. Between the time of their having registered on this cut and now some things had changed, i.e., the weather had become overcast and damp, which affected the propelling charges and air density. Fortunately for us, these changes created overs and shorts at the same elevation, thus causing shells to hit the tops of this cut. The enemy could not move his elevation even one mill and hit us.

Each time one of these shells exploded overhead and on top of the opposite side of this cut, our tank rocked. Shrapnel also sailed harmlessly over our heads. After the first couple of rounds, the driver and gunner jumped out of the tank following me into the stone house from which our Task Force Commander was directing his attack. These two enlisted men had not been ordered to stay at their posts in our tank as had Sgt. T—, leaving the Sgt. alone. Why these men felt more secure inside the old stone house instead of in our tank, I could not imagine.

Having delivered my message to the Colonel, I awaited his reply. He carefully penned his answer and gave it to me and so I headed for the door. Suddenly confronting me at the door was Sgt. T—. I recall opening my mouth to bawl him out for leaving his post, but not a sound came out of me. The look on his face stopped me cold, his eyes were glassy, his face dead white and his whole body was trembling.

What I did next was far beyond my training or experience, for it came like a flash from "on high". Realizing that a lone man inside a tank being rocked by repeated near and heavy explosions was cause for a good case of claustrophobia, I laid my hand on Sgt. T—'s arm and quietly said, "I'll get back into the tank with you." The Sgt.'s eyes began to focus once more and he relaxed as if a huge weight had been lifted from his shoulders. At that I turned to the rest of my crew and shouted, "Let's go!".

As we raced out doors toward our tank, another salvo screamed in. We hit the dirt. Again it was split over and shorts exploding harmlessly high overhead on both sides of the cut. We all scrambled into the turret and I roared into the intercom, "Move out fast!". Then I looked up at that dense overcast sky. it was 1100 hours and I knew somewhere above, the sun was shining brightly, which meant soon the air beneath those clouds would dry just a tad, with two results. First, the enemy's propelling charges would dry somewhat and this would increase their range slightly. Second, the air density would thin a bit and this would decrease their range a little. Consequently these differences would then be enough to drop those shells exactly into the cut. We had not moved sixty yards at an ever increasing speed when looking back I saw the next salvo hit the cut exactly at the spot we had just vacated. Wow!

Sgt. T— was one of the best men I have ever known. He was certainly a fine young American by any standard. He always did his job quietly and efficiently, nor did he ever complain. He was also a self-starter. He served out the war without difficulty. Except for that one brief moment cited as above when I believe his mind hung by a slender thread, his service was flawless. I count it as a gift of God that I was granted the correct thing to do and say which helped him see past that very traumatic moment. In no way do I claim credit for this insight; it was beyond my comprehension and in the hands of a "greater power".

I am sure that after all these years, Sgt. T— will forgive me for sharing this moment of truth. I have neither seen nor heard from him for nearly forty-eight years. He undoubtedly returned to civilian life after the War and is now probably holding his grand-children on his knee. I wish him well always, wherever he is.

This particular case was only one of three times that General Morris and I used heavy tanks forward of Division Headquarters; usually we or I traveled by jeep. On the occasion of crossing the Saar River before the Siegfried Line on the Ninety Fourth Infantry Division's pontoon bridge, we used an armored car. We should have used a jeep then as shells were exploding overhead and our column was forced to halt for some time. We sat midstream hoping the enemy shrapnel would not find us. As most of you know, an armored car has an open top and with shells bursting overhead it was no more protection than an open jeep. I have always believed that using an armored car was inadvisable since it had no more overhead protection than a jeep.

Our Light Tank

Gen. Morris   Lt. Chapman

18
Advanced Command Post

In all Armored Divisions in World War II, the Division Command Post was usually divided into two headquarter sections called "forward" and "rear". On this one particular occasion, General Morris established an "Advanced Command Post" which consisted of himself, G-2, G-3 and me plus a minimum number of drivers and radio signal people as required. Also included were five M.P.s. Altogether there were two medium tanks, two half-tracks (G-2 and G-3), three jeeps and one 3/4 ton truck for the M.P.s. This number was deemed necessary as our Combat Command A and Combat Command B had made such fast time in their attacks through enemy resistance that they were about fifteen miles ahead of even our forward Command Post. It was dark and to move the Forward Command Post during darkness would take too long and continuity might be lost. They could have moved better the next day, but nevertheless our little caravan headed off into the darkness. Terrain was quite hilly and heavily wooded. We proceeded several miles and were about four miles behind our forward elements when we came across a wood cutter's house by the roadside. It was unoccupied and General Morris decided to spend the balance of the night here as we had excellent radio communication with both our Combat Commands and the Forward Division Command Post, justifying his reasons to create this Advance Command Post. Radio contact between the attacking elements which were continuing to attack all night and the Division Forward Command Post had become so faint as to be difficult or nearly impossible due largely to mountain terrain.

As we moved the two half-tracks next to this stone wood cutter's house for convenience in transmitting, one of our Divison infantrymen, Sergeant Eugene F. McFarland, appeared and asked us if we could take over the guarding of fifty Krauts (P.O.W.'s) he had near by. Immediately I said "no" and questioned him further. He said that he and one other G.I., Private Wilbur McCullen, were holding the prisoners in a ground depression about one hundred feet behind the house. I investigated and found his story to be true and so I notified the G-2. I also sent one of our M.P.'s to help guard the P.O.W.'s. Sergeant McFarland and Private McCullen could not understand why I was not willing to take these prisoners off their hands nor did I explain.

Shortly thereafter something happened which really raised the hair on our heads. Aided by moon light, we could see what appeared to be a German Infantry Company marching in squad column across this secondary road, not two hundred yards from our location!

Being responsible for the safety of all present, I immediately directed several measures to be taken. As I was sure the enemy knew there was an armored unit at this house due to the whine and talk on several radios and the noise of our armor moving in, I relocated the vehicles circling them like old wagon trains in the U.S. West. Next to the house two half-tracks presented their front end toward the Germans, next the tanks moved in and then completing our circle were three jeeps and a 3/4 ton truck. All vehicles had thirty or fifty machine guns manned by drivers or assistant drivers. The main tank guns were sighted down the road toward the visible enemy troops. All windows in the first floor of this house were barricaded with heavy furniture piled against its windows. I stationed the remaining four M.P.'s at these openings and a few of the other men at upstairs windows.

I then hiked over to the P.O.W. area and had our men make the Krauts either to lie face down or sit with their head on their knees in the lowest land depression. Sergeant McFarland and Private McCullen were to shoot at any noise or movement of the P.O.W.'s; now they learned my strategy.

Returning quickly to the house, I climbed into one of the tanks switching to the Division Artillery net. Relying on my previous experience as a field artillery forward observer, I advised our Division Artillery the target and coordinates — "will adjust, over". The repy came back — "Roger — wait, over". Shortly came their answer, "Artillery in defilade. Cannot hit this target area. Over and out". Knowing that the General would never agree to turning around a team to come back to our aid, and that the only other friendly troops were the Division's Trains about twenty miles behind us, we were definitely on our own.

Had the German Commander realized our true situation and that there were fifty of his own soldiers as P.O.W.'s nearby, he certainly would have attacked us. We could only hope that they had a "belly full" of our earlier armored thrust and wanted to clear the area as fast as possible.

So this was another night no one got any sleep, for good
reason!

19
Ayl, Germany

A new overcoat was a tough item to come by during combat. I did not have an officer's trench coat all winter long in 1944. At times the weather was down to ten degrees F. Other days were warmer but never over thirty four degrees. So without a good overcoat I felt cold often.

When I heard that Captain Smith of Division Headquarters was to go to Paris in February 1945, I approached him with my request to purchase a new coat. The price was $50.00. He graciously agreed to do so if possible. On 22 February, Captain Smith returned with my coat. It was really a red letter day for me!

On the 23rd, Division Headquarters was moved to Ayl, Germany where it stayed until the 26th. The headquarters was located in a two story building facing the river and only a short distance from it. Just before daylight on the 24th, another officer and I came out the front door past the M.P. guard and walked over to my jeep located a few feet away. I deposited my new coat on the back of the jeep and we walked around the corner of the building to the rear where a slit trench latrine had been dug inside a shed. The two of us had just entered this shed when a Kraut 88 shell hit the front of the headquarters building. This one shell did a lot of damage. It killed Major Barns, Headquarters Commander, Sergeant Claus, our jeep driver, and several others. In addition, it wounded seriously our M.P.

guard, Corporal James Gralick, Colonel Thayer, our Chief of Staff and others. My jeep was destroyed as well. When I picked up my new coat, it looked like a piece of Belgian lace. I was very happy not to have been inside it when the shell burst. So much for my new $50.00 coat!

An adjunct to this story was the joke originated by Colonel Shefield to the effect that, "Had I not been sitting down when the shell burst, it would have blown my head off." It always is good to have a sense of humor at such times.

The other officer who had been in the latrine at the same time jumped when the shell burst, striking his ear against the stone wall. The gash bled profusely and nothing we could do would stop the bleeding. So he walked over to our aid station. They not only patched up his ear but gave him a "Purple Heart". We both had many a chuckle about this later.

20
The Bridge

Task Force Richardson roared into the outskirts of Trier before dawn on 1 March, 1945. Its task was to capture intact three bridges which crossed the Moselle River at Trier. The two modern steel structures were blown up by the Nazis just as we reached their approaches. On the left flank of Task Force Richardson was Lieutenant Riley of the Eleventh Tank Battalion and with his team of infantry and light tanks. We remember those old light tanks and referred to them as buckets of bolts. They mounted a 37 mm. main gun and a .30 caliber machine gun. The label "bucket of bolts" came about because they were constructed of light armor plate riveted together.

When Team Riley arrived at an old stone bridge, it was still intact. Without hesitation, he ordered Lieutenant Wilbur Beadle's Platoon of tanks to take the bridge. Thereupon Beadle ordered his first Section to the right of the bridge and Second Section to the left. They were to fire machine guns across the river to prevent any Krauts from approaching the bridge from the other side. Lieutenant Beadle then ran the bridge in his tank and, firing his machine gun, intercepted a German Major just as he was about to put his hand on the detonator. As a result the bridge was saved and Task Force Richardson quickly established a bridge-head on the German side of the Moselle in Trier

It seems that this old stone bridge, called the Romer

bridge, had been built by Caesar's Tenth Roman Legion seventeen centuries before and now was "saved" by Patton's Tenth Armored Division. The next day our Division's engineers removed ten thousand 1/4 lb. charges from this old stone bridge.

We had taken several bridges before in combat and would again, but this bridge was unique for several reasons. It was truly a piece of history. Secondly, and by far the more important from our point of view, it enabled the Third Army to flank the entire western wall of Germany's defenses. At that time their defensive line extended from the Netherlands in the north to the anchor of Trier in the south. The German Army had dug in all along this line and on ground of their own choosing. It was a formidable line. All the Allied Armies were attempting to attack and penetrate it but were getting nowhere. Certainly the Allies could have broken through it in time but the loss of life would have been very great. Now it was no longer necessary to do so as our flanking action had turned the end of their defensive line. Most military historians do not give sufficient credit to our Division's turning this Nazi's flank anchor. It is my opinion that this action of ours shortened the war by about three months, since the Nazis had to fall back to the Rhine River. During their retreat, all Allied Armies attacked them and with our Air Corp the Nazi army suffered. It lost thousands of killed, wounded, and captured along with major losses in artillery and tanks. By the time it has crossed the Rhine River, it was the beginning of the end of the Third Reich. Tough and deadly battles were yet to be fought but never again could Hitler present such formidable defenses.

Not enough good can be said about Lieutenant Beadle and

his tank crew who took the risk during dawn's early light, in running that bridge. Heroes all, I am certain they never fully comprehended the handsome pay-off to our overall cause. Their one act undoubtedly saved many thousands of allied lives and shortened the war by months.

21
The Behemoths

There are three ways to defend a defile: at the entrance, in the defile, and at the exit. The Nazi chose to defend the exit so when our first tanks rumbled out of the mountain exit onto the flat Rhine River plain, "it" hit us.

We did not know what "it" was nor could anyone see what or from where "it" was shooting. The lead Task Force commander had ordered his medium tanks to lead his column through this defile. Immediately upon exiting the defile, the three lead tanks were completely demolished and the entire column stopped. Listening on the radio, I knew something really important had occurred, but due to the excited talk and lack of firm data, the message made little sense to me. At this junction, the Task Force Commander ordered his Armored Infantry forward out onto the plain. I dismounted and ran forward with elements of our infantry as far as the "exit" to the plain. There were three little rural villages, each about 3000 yards from this "exit" looking sleepy and peaceful in the morning sun. Surveying our three destroyed tanks, I was awed. They must have been hit by some extremely heavy solid shot as their turrets were thrown about fifty feet away from their frames and these frames were sliced through from front to rear laying the tanks open like a peeled banana. Their engines, of course, were broken apart. One projectile had not only destroyed a tank but torn down a stone house behind it and continued on burying itself deep into a hill side.

Our Task Force Commander had quickly taken a back azimuth and determined that the fire was coming from the village on our left and so ordered the infantry with mortars forward to attack the village. No one could see a weapon yet, but as our troops approached the village in typical spread out formation running and flopping down, we suddenly saw a huge tank coming out of a barn for, the Krauts had backed their monsters into barns or ground floors of several houses. To those not familiar with European peasant villages, whether they be French, German or Polish, the ground floor is the barn for animals, while the second story is where people live and the third story is for storing hay, grain, and dried fruits. By backing their tanks into the barn and closing the door, these tanks were not visible to us and they only opened a door long enough to fire and then slammed it shut again.

This first enemy tank stopped and fired at one of our anti-tank guns cutting it in half and killing its crew. Our infantry then noticed this tank crew exited the rear of their tank to load and ram home another round. Before the Krauts could load again, our infantry dropped a few "little" 60 mm. mortar rounds around this tank thus killing its crew. All at once five more of these large tanks appeared out of barns. At this juncture, our Task Force Commander ordered his entire armored force to thunder out of the "exit" and at full speed toward this village in fanned out formation. One of our tanks hit one of these huge German tanks frontally with a solid shot, which did no damage at all and merely glanced off. Another of our tanks caught one of theirs moving across his field of fire. Our tank's solid shot against the side of that tank destroyed it completely. By noon, all six of these monsters were either destroyed or captured.

What were those German tanks like? The frontal section of its fixed turret was six inches thick of good steel on a 30 degree angle. It mounted a six inch naval gun which had to be loaded and rammed by its crew opening two steel doors on the back side, dismounting and hand ramming. The main gun could only traverse right or left two degrees from center before it became necessary to start the engine and turn the entire vehicle. The treads were forty two inches wide and the entire tank weighed one hundred tons.

To my way of thinking, this tank was an "armored gun" and not a true tank because of its fixed turret and means of loading. Additionally, it had the best optics I ever looked through; the gunner could split hairs at 3000 yards! There were only six of these monsters in the Nazi arsenal. It was obvious when the Krauts saw our infantry attack coming at them they had to move out because they had no infantry at hand to defend these "Yak Tiger Tanks", which we incorrectly called them. They should have been called "Jodl" tanks named after German General Jodl, who was their army's ordinance expert.

This success was one more first for our Tenth Armored Division.

22
Orchards

Standing in the old ruined schloss or castle above Heidelberg, Germany, I watched the initial phases of our attack progress southward below me. Our task forces were moving steadily across the Neckar River's plains through the peach and apple orchards against heavy enemy fire, including many 88's. After the initial phase began, I climbed into our medium tank and proceeded down to the orchards to follow the lead task force. General Morris had sent me to observe this attack while he did the same with another task force further east.

Due to the intensity of small arms fire, we "buttoned up" our tank and its driver used his periscope to drive. Artillery fire began arriving thick and fast. Suddenly, the tank stopped; I called to the driver on the intercom but received no answer so I repeated the question, "Why did we stop?". There was no answer. I asked the gunner to have a look at the driver through the dog house or exit door under the 75 mm. gun. He reported that the driver was slumped over in his seat. I climbed out of the turret and personally crawled through the door under the main gun and into the driver's compartment. The motor was running at idle speed and all seemed to be in good order except that blood was dripping from the driver's limp hand. Then I saw that the chop of the last shell had burst and ruptured the periscope and hit our driver in the face, killing him instantly.

I ordered all hatches open and shut off the motor.

Together the three of us — gunner, loader and I lifted our friend out of his seat and laid him gently on the grounds. Wiping the seat area, we proceeded on our mission.

It was indeed a sad day for all of us for this driver was one of the best. His physical appearance belied his strength for I have seen him with one hand pick up a twelve pound sledge on the end of the handle opposite the head and in one hard blow knock loose a pin connecting the tank tread. Very calmly he would then pick up the free end of the tread lifting it over his shoulder and "walking the tread" off the idlers.

He was a brave and courageous young man who quietly did his job without fanfare and was a true credit to our Division. I regret I can not recall his name.

23

Heilbronn - Ashes and the Phoenix

Those of you who were there will vividly recall our approach in 1945 to Heilbronn. It was a beautiful city of limestone houses with flower boxes at most windows and grand public buildings and paved streets with a population of about one hundred thousand. It was also considered one of the gateways to the Nazi "Redoubt Area". Other cities in this classification in our area were Crailsheim and Ulm.

As our lead units approached Heilbronn, all the windows were open in every building facing us. From past experience, we immediately sensed danger and so proceeded into the edge of town with great caution. Our men had not penetrated more than one hundred yards when machine gun and panzer foust fire greeted us from out of those empty windows. We had met the Nazi's Seventeenth S.S. Division. Our Commander immediately pulled back out of town and our Division's Artillery opened up with a McCabe "Heat Treatment". Our Four Hundred Nineteenth Armored Field Artillery Battalion Commander Lieutenant Colonel McCabe had created this "Heat Treatment" for just such an occasion. It consisted of five hundred rounds of white phosphorous and five hundred rounds of high explosive shells. Following this phase, our tank infantry task forces opened up with everything they had on the enemy now ensconced in the city.

Earlier, Heilbronn had suffered one fire bomb air attack

by British Bristol night bombers, burning several large buildings in the center of town. Remaining buildings were unharmed until our ground attack began. The S.S. troops plus members of Hitler's Youth Corp fought desperately as Hitler ordered them to fight to the last man to stop our attack.

In Von Uwe Jacob's book, Die Vermisten Ratsprotokolle, written circa 1948-1950, concerning this period, he pointedly makes reference to the fact that the S.S. troops placed the young boys of "Hitler's Youth" (fourteen to sixteen) in front of them. They either fought or the S.S. shot them. He recounts that one youngster was so scared that he threw his arms around one of the S.S. men and begged for his life. These boys were directed to shoot at and scream at our tanks, but with all the gunfire, they were scarcely heard.

We would attack a stone house or public building by blowing a hole in the wall then firing automatic weapons and tank guns through the hole and into the openings. Our infantry then threw hand grenades into the building and rushed in with guns blazing. As soon as we cleared out a building, the Seventeenth S.S. stormed it also from the other side by blowing holes in it using their panzer fousts. Then they stormed it. Each and every house and building changed hands three or four times in as many hours. In between times our troops fought hand to hand combat with the S.S. troops.

Corp Commander decided that after seeing the determined resistance of the enemy that it would be better for our Division to be replaced by the One Hundredth Infantry Division and so we were pulled out and ordered to the city of Ulm. The actual Heilbronn battle lasted nine days from 3 to 12

April, 1945. Our Division fought there about two days during that period before being ordered out.

Before our Division arrived and attached Heilbronn, several very interesting things happened. It seems that the Mayor of this fair city wanted to save it and the people from further war devastation so he ordered white flags to be hung out of open windows. Most of the people left this city of 100,000 civilians. Only about 800 remained, their reason being: Germany could not win the war and it was senseless to destroy their city and die trying to save it. When the Seventeenth S.S. Division arrived with orders to defend it, the Nazi general countermanded the Mayor's order. There was a big argument at the Mayor's home between the Mayor and the General. At this juncture, a high ranking Nazi by the name of Richard Drauz joined the argument. He ordered the Mayor shot as a traitor. The General agreed and did so in the Mayor's own home and in front of his family.

Down the street a ways from the Mayor's home lived another German civilian by the name of Karl Traubenberger. The Germans had built a tank trap between a church and a house in which a woman and her small child lived. The neighbors felt that if the American Tenth Armored Division was to attack this trap, they would probably plow through their house, killing or injuring the woman and her child. This would have been the way around the trap, so her neighbors decided to remove the tank trap. Traubenberger told them to stop because he knew Drauz, a Nazi official, wanted the tank trap left in place. When the Nazi Drauz heard about the commotion, he ordered both Traubenberger and the woman picked up and brought before him at Nazi headquarters.

Both Traubenberger and the young woman were accused of treason and ordered shot, their bodies to be left in the street. Traubenberger attempted to explain that he tried to stop the people from destroying the tank trap. Traubenberger was then shot and his body left in the street with a sign "I am a traitor!" around his neck. The young woman somehow fled in the confusion. The tank trap remained. Meanwhile two or three other citizens defied the Nazis' order and placed white flags at their windows. Drauz and the Seventeenth S.S. General had these citizens hunted down and dragged out into the street and shot, leaving their bodies as a sign that whosoever defied the Nazis would meet the same end. As the battle for Heilbronn raged on, these Nazis would meet the same end. During the battle for Heilbronn, these same Nazis blew up large buildings so they could not be used by the Americans as shelter or fortresses. They also blew up all the bridges across the Neckar River.

It must be told that after all the fighting was over and the Third Reich surrendered, Richard Drauz and his wife changed their names to Richard Binder and disappeared on 15 April, 1945. They left three children with friends or relatives in Tubenberger. Binder and his wife, using forged I.D. papers, then fled to Dernbach where he obtained a job as a gardener in a monastery. She worked as a helper in a nearby hospital. It was here that our Counter Intelligence Corp arrested Drauz (Binder) on 15 July, 1945. On 4 December, Drauz was found guilty of war crimes, i.e. killing of surrendered G.I.'s on 24 March of that same year. He was hanged by the neck immediately at Landsberg, Germany.

In Von Uwe Jacobi's book he tells in detail much that the Nazis did to their own people which none of the Americans knew. His book is a collection of eyewitness accounts given freely in investigative reporting on Heilbronn during the Nazi period 1933-1945. Much of my understanding of this German account comes from Mrs. Crystall Williams who translated the book into English. Crystall was a young teenager in Berlin during the War; her father despised Hitler and his thugs. At War's end, their house was located fortunately in West Berlin. I thank her for this help.

At the end of the battle for Heilbronn, I returned briefly to the exact location where we had entered that unfortunate city. Its desolation was total. Great piles of rubble stretched as far as the eye could see in all directions. Iron water pipes protruded upward above the debris with their upper ends twisted into grotesque shapes. Here and there a splintered chimney corner staggered drunkenly skyward. The pungent, dank odor of death assaulted my nostrils from every quarter. Who were these dead: a woman with her child; an old man and his faithful dog; a neighbor's cat; plus many soldiers - both theirs and ours. All had been buried beneath the rubble. Lucky were the ones who died instantly. Others were caught by falling mortar and stone - held more tightly than any jail could do. These died slowly from thirst and crushed and fractured bones.

To my ears came the scurry of tiny feet. Rats - those most despised creatures! Could one blame them? No, they were nature's sanitation squads. They burrowed deep within the rubble and dined upon decaying flesh. Alone I stood — feet rooted; mind sick and with sight dimmed by salty tears shed for our fallen comrades. My only companion was the mournful wind as it moved through the wreckage. Heilbronn was truly a city of the dead!

Quoting the "Stars and Stripes": The One Hundredth Infantry Division under General W.A. Burress stated "Heilbronn was a second Bitche". (Bitche was a stronghold on the Maginot Line in Elsass and it took the One Hundredth Division three months to defeat it.) His troops drove the S.S. out of that destroyed city. Correspondent Howard Bryne tells this story: "The basement rooms in a house in Heilbronn were full of dust and dirt. The house shook and the faces of the soldiers were red and sweaty. Shooting upsets one's stomach and shakes a building. The city had already been taken and was now occupied for our forces. We were told after breakfast. Sergeant Derwall said, "I think we are still on this side of the Neckar Bridge". "I thought Bitche was a terrible scene but this is a son of a bitch", groaned Sergeant Ross. Some of the men of the One Hundredth Infantry Division laughed to relieve their tension.

Quoting again from Uwe Jacobi's book: "Fear gripped the citizens of Heilbonn in March, 1945 as Americans were approaching their city. People fled to safety in forests, railroad tunnels, and air raid shelters. Few remained in the city. Two mothers with their small children huddled in the corner of a barn as the G.I.'s arrived. They were hoping not to be found as the Nazi's had told them what beasts Americans were and especially our black soldiers. Two G.I.'s entered the barn and brought them and their children out. The women were trembling with fear. A black G.I. motioned a child to come to him whereupon he gave the child a big hug then walked away. The women were certainly relieved!" Then our troops moved on and one more Nazi lie was destroyed.

I have not been back since that fateful day so long ago. Word has reached me that as the populous slowly returned they began to remove the city's rubble. After all the local German P.O.W.'s were freed in 1947, they joined other citizens of Heilbronn to begin rebuilding their city. Today it is almost as it was prior to that devastating 1945 battle.

Heilbronn, Germany
April 1945

Main Street
Heilbronn, Germany

24
Crailsheim, Germany

Our Division was attempting to get a foothold into the gateway city of Crailsheim, Germany. Like Ulm and Heilbronn, Crailsheim was considered one of those cities that were entrances into the German Redoubt of Bavaria which the Nazi intended to hold at all cost — down to the last man! More detailed encounters are clearly set forth in our Division's book Impact (pages 219-249) by Lester Nickles. A few interesting events were omitted, however, but I would like now to relate them to you.

One of the first casualties to be flown out of Crailsheim was Lieutenant Colonel Ned Norris. He was near me when hit on 8 April, 1945. Earlier that morning, I had seen him jump from a shed roof onto a German soldier, knocking him to the ground. By the time they had hit the dirt, Colonel Norris had slit the German's throat with that razor sharp knife he always carried. Whereupon, Colonel Norris immediately swung about firing his .45 into the shed from which the Hun had emerged. There were others inside who came stumbling out with their hands up and surrendered to the Colonel.

In spite of the rather somber or even pessimistic feeling one gets by reading in Impact the account of Crailsheim, Lieutenant Colonel "Red" Hankins told me recently that our Division could have stayed longer in Crailsheim. After one of the German attacks on his position, he said that he had walked over the ground where the German dead had fallen. The entire "battle plan" was evident to his practiced eye as the enemy soldiers had fallen in their exact attack positions, indicating clearly that our artillery, mortar, machine guns, along with our tank fire, had done their job expertly.

To me, there seemed to be three key situations that made Crailsheim similar to Bastogne. First, our route into both cities was on roads or low ground as compared to the hills along both flanks. The enemy did not hold this high ground at first because our brilliant attack completely surprised them. When they discovered what we were up to, they seized, held and occupied this higher hill ground. The enemy's speedy and intense build-up of troops and continuous flank attacks on our positions and supply columns required an almost constant re-taking of key points and villages.

Second, after Colonel "Red" Hankins' men had taken the airfield, General Piburn of Combat Command A sent our Fifty Fifth Engineers to clear the airfield of burned out German planes, 88 guns and trucks, and also to fill bomb craters. Our Ninth Troop Carrier Command re-supplied the men of Combat Command A with needed rations of fuel, arms and food. Their men evacuated our wounded on return trips. It was incumbent upon our ground troops in the Crailsheim area to neutralize enemy 88's, artillery and mortar fire so re-supply efforts would be successful. In doing so, the air command lost only one plane.

The third concern of our men and commanding officers was the almost continuous attack by German troops upon us, day and night. Fresh German battalions and regiments of engineers and infantry were thrown into this battle as soon as they arrived from the north, south and east. Their onslaught had a wearing effect upon us not unlike Bastogne's.

The Sixth Corp, realizing that our brilliant surprise attack could not be followed up due to our lack of infantry and intense enemy air and ground action, ordered us out of the Crailsheim area on 11 April, 1945. While this battle was disappointing to our command due to the fact that we were unable to make a complete breakthrough by capturing a bridge over the Neckar River, our withdrawal cannot be considered a true defeat. Our Division captured two thousand men and killed one thousand of the enemy. At the same time, we had held the airfield and Crailsheim. Our gunners had shot down many enemy planes and greatly weakened the enemy's future ability to resist. There was more enemy air action over us than anywhere on the entire western front during this operation, because they used the M.E.-109's and their new jets (M.E.-262) fighters. It is to be noted that fifty of these attacking planes were shot down by our small arms and anti-aircraft fire. This was one fourth of those enemy planes.

25
Ulm, Germany

"History often repeats itself", it is said. Sometimes it is repeated at the convenience of politicians! My example supports this claim.

Our Tenth Armored Division was in the Seventh Army and Six Corp in 1945. The Corp had ordered our Division to drive on Ulm and take it. Ulm was one of those gateway cities to the redoubt area of Bavaria which the Nazis had determined to hold to the last man, i.e. no quarter was to be given nor asked. Their Seventeenth S.S. Division had holed up in Ulm with their "do or die" orders.

Ulm was at the junction of the Danube River and a canal. The Danube at this point is about twelve feet wide and fordable at least at one location.

While our Tenth Armored Division was still some ten or fifteen miles away from Ulm, we located this ford and proceeded across it posting an infantry guard on each bank. During the night the First French Armored Division came to the ford. This unit had mounted on top of their tanks an Algerian Ghum regiment whose men wore long, loose white flowing robes. Besides American General Sherman tanks, this French Armored Unit included French and German trucks, cars and American jeeps plus an assortment of German and French artillery. None of the Algerians could speak French or English and the French officers could not speak English. Not knowing what to do as no one could communicate, our guards called their sergeant who decided that in as much as they were our allies, we should let them pass through the ford. Accordingly, they were passed through. This was not reported to higher commanders.

Night was falling rapidly and soon a very dark night settled upon us. There was no moon and stars were obscured most of the time by cloud cover. Towards morning, another military column approached the ford. Due to the darkness and because it had a mix of various types of military vehicles, our guards merely waved it through the ford. This column turned out to be entirely German, however. Further up the road this column was stopped by a blown bridge over the canal. Our Tenth Armored Division engineers were working with a bulldozer preparing the approach for pontoon bridging. The German column stopped and their captain got out and asked, "Vas ist loss?". Whereupon all hell broke out as everybody was shooting at everyone else.

In the darkness, American G.I.'s were running with German Infantry and vice versa. Our Division's G-2 told us later that he realized that the two men he was running beside were Germans. He dropped onto one knee from where he could make out the shape of their helmets and he shot them both with his .45 cal. pistol. For some reason one of the other Germans crawled under a bulldozer during shooting and our engineer dropped the blade on him, another dead Kraut! When all the shooting stopped and daylight arrived, the few remaining Krauts were rounded up immediately.

It was then the main body of the French First Armored Division, with the Algerians aboard, ran out of fuel for their tanks and trucks. The French had deliberately turned left ninety degrees out of their designated army area and were well into our American Seventh zone. They had not only disobeyed their orders from S.H.A.E.F., but had by-passed a considerable German force which they were to have invested and destroyed. All this effort was spent trying to take Ulm just because Napoleon had done so many years before. The German column that forded the Danube was part of the enemy forces which the French should have attacked and destroyed, but for the French the capture of Ulm took precedence.

General Morris, Commanding General of our Tenth Armored Division, immediately reported by radio this violation of orders by the French to General Brooks our Six Corp Commander. Upon hearing this report, General Brooks was furious and ordered General Morris to attack the French and destroy "those S.O.B.'s". General Morris replied that he would proceed to neutralize them at once. At this juncture, a delegation consisting of the Commanding General of the French Armored Division and the Regimental Commander of the Algerian Regiment arrived to see General Morris. They needed fuel and artillery ammunition to continue their attack on Ulm which was about ten miles ahead. Our Division had a French Lieutenant assigned to us from the time we entered France, and so General Morris called for him to come and interpret. The French and our interpreter talked in French as to how and what should be said to General Morris about their needs. Finally a statement of request was given in English to General Morris. He replied courteously that he would have to check with his higher Corp to be able to meet their requests. Giving them a carton of cigarettes, he dismissed them with a promise to let them know as soon as he would hear. As soon as the liaison officer (translator) and the French Army representatives were out of hearing range, General Morris called in the G-3 and ordered double guards to be posted day and night on all our vehicles and supply dumps. In no case were we to give any fuel, food, or ammunition to the French. This order effectively isolated them without spilling blood as General Brooks would have had us do.

Then General Morris broke out laughing. As I could see nothing funny, I asked him what was so hilarious? After he calmed down, he said that he was a past master at speaking French and he understood everything they had said in his presence. He kept a straight face, which he could do very well, so as not to tip his hand.

The battle for Ulm was started by our Division and partway through the house-to-house fighting, our Corp sent in an infantry division to relieve us so we could make an "end run" around Ulm. After the American Infantry destroyed the city, S.H.A.E.F. intervened and ordered the First French Armored Division, with the Algerian troops, to relieve our Infantry Division and complete the job of killing the last platoon of enemy soldiers so they (the French) could raise their Tri-Colors over Ulm for political (Napoleonic) reasons.

The French Army never really took Ulm. We Americans did so with our blood and sacrifice and should have been given credit for the action in the history books.

This nefarious scheme to claim victory over Ulm was initiated by DeGaulle to give him political credibility with his

countrymen. Upon this half-truth and many others, DeGaulle
was to build his post-war political machine. To indicate just how
impossible it would have been for the French to capture Ulm,
allow me to set forth some little known information.

First, the French Armor and Infantry Division, due to
their lack of fuel and ammunition, was stalled six or seven miles
from Ulm. All of the Seventh U.S. Army, Six U.S. Corp, and our
Tenth Armored Division were mad as hell at the French because
they had deliberately violated their orders from S.H.A.E.F. to
fight in their French Army zone and to destroy a large body of
German troops there. Instead, they by-passed these enemy
units, turned left ninety degrees out of their zone and went deep
into our Seventh Army zone towards Ulm. This took them
several miles north and they wound up directly in our Tenth
Armored Division's easterly path. This change of plan was made
without either advising or asking permission and the first our
Division ran into the French Armor was short of Ulm as
indicated above. At that point the French tanks and artillery
fired upon our Division thinking we were German troops. How
they could have made that mistake was absolutely incredible!
All they really had to do was look. We had the same type tanks
and half-tracks as they did, but emblazoned on all sides and top
of our vehicles were the large white stars of the U.S. Army. That
day was clear and bright with visibility unlimited. They did not
stop firing until we sent their French liaison officer, who had
been attached to our Division's Headquarters, to them in a jeep
to tell them to cease firing. It was a double tragedy for us, for
some of our men and officers were wounded or killed and several
vehicles were damaged. Those French must have been both

blind and dumb not to recognize us as Americans. We gave all tanks, half-tracks, and artillery to them plus fuel and ammunition. The very shells we had given them were now returned to us in a murderous fashion. Besides, they should have known that Seventh Army troops would be advancing eastward in our own zone.

It should be pointed out that some years after the close of World War II an article appeared in the Reader's Digest stating that the French had captured Ulm. I wrote begging to differ and stated the true facts as above. Its reply was to the same effect as the article with the added notation that they had checked with the DeGaulle French Government. Naturally, he was not about to admit to a political "cover up".

The second reason the French could not have really taken Ulm was that two U.S. Divisions did. First our Tenth Armored Division began and then a U.S. Infantry Division finished the job. The Americans had captured all of Ulm except one stone building with about thirty enemy inside it before Eisenhower ordered the Americans to stop the attack, give fuel and ammunition to the French stopped outside of Ulm, and pass French forces through our lines to storm the last remnants of the German Army. In the meantime, our Tenth Armored Division had pulled out of Ulm after we had turned the city over to our U.S. Infantry friends and swung around behind Ulm, destroying enemy artillery and supply routes. Also, we chopped up their infantry reserves as they tried to come to the aid of their fellow embattled German troops. At this junction, the U.S. Infantry Commander had two options. First, he could merely wait for the Germans to run out of food, water, and ammunition, which would take only a couple of days as they were in low supply of these items. Our Tenth Armored Division had already slammed the door shut on their re-supply so their position was hopeless. Second, his troops could have vigorously continued the attack; in about four hours more they would have taken Ulm. Before a decision had been made, General Eisenhower's order arrived and thus deprived our U.S. forces of total victory at Ulm.

It has never been my purpose in any way to disparage the French people. They have been and still are great engineers, and scientists as well as marvelous artists and writers. Sometime between 1940 and 1943, General Charles DeGaulle crossed over from being a great soldier-patriot of France to becoming a politician. In this later phase of his life, he dismissed the chance to be a truly magnanimous world leader, as he concentrated on the narrower acts of self-interest while disguising it as the interest of France. It's just another instance where politics outweighed military tactics. Churchill said it best, "Of all the crosses I have to bear, the Cross of Lorraine is the heaviest".

26
Drums

When our Division captured Kaiserslautern with its extensive railroad yards, our Division's troops discovered these yards had several interesting railway features.

First, these rail yards were a major marshaling and staging facility for southern Germany, Switzerland, and the Provinces of Alsace and Lorraine.

Second, there were train loads - not just a few freight cars - but entire train loads of goods stolen from homes and castles all over Europe. The Nazis had pulled these trains onto rail sidings so they could sort out their loot and decide where to ship it. In one train would be found sterling table service. One box would have a set of twenty-four complete place settings with the rightful owner's crest and initials on each piece. Another box, contained a set of fifty, yet another set of only twelve. And so it went throughout one entire train. Another entire train would have many sterling silver coffee and tea sets. Each set would also have its rightful owner's crest or initials. With every box being different as to content and ownership. The next train might be all linens. One could open a box and find an exquisite lace trimmed linen table cloth with twenty-four matching napkins. Another box might contain luncheon table cloths with matching napkins. Some sets had their owner's initials on their corners. Another train could contain oil paintings and water colors. I always believed that practically all of this loot was stolen from Jews and anyone who crossed the Nazis. I presumed most of these rightful owners would never be located.

Third, in one of the railroad sheds was located the drum and pipes of the Gordon Highlander Regimental Band. It seems that this Band was forced to leave these instruments at Dunkirk in May and June of 1940 when the British evacuated Europe through Dunkirk.

Our Division immediately advised the Third Army of this discovery and they relayed this information to Supreme Allied Headquarters and they in turn to the British government. We immediately received a reply stating that the entire Gordon Highland Regimental Band was on its way to collect its instruments. General Morris ordered a large field to be cleared and checked as safe from anti-personnel and land mines. This field was adjacent to the railroad yards on one side and a bombed out section of Kaiserslauten on the other. This project took place between 20 and 23 March, 1945. A ceremony to mark the return of these instruments was planned on short notice. I believe our Division's band was involved along with one or more platoons of armored infantry; just which units were involved I do not recall. After these instruments were presented to our kilted friends dressed in their fancy dress uniforms, they played old Scottish airs for about forty minutes. At the first sound of the pipes, German civilians began crawling out of every hole and broken cellar and stood atop the city's ruins to watch and listen. Some of our men were a bit concerned and swung their machine guns on our vehicles around to cover these civilians. No worry - they were only curious and enjoyed a welcome relief - music!

We stood enraptured by such songs as: "You Take the

High Road and I'll Take the Low Road and I'll Get To Scotland Before Ye"; "Old Bard", and many more. For a short spell, I was emotionally whisked away to other times and places of long ago. I could see in my mind's eye the early morning mist rising above Loch Lomond, obscuring the beautiful broken irregular hills behind which shrill pipes sent their pleading notes across the land.

At the end of their short concert, the "Ladies From Hell" climbed into their trucks and returned. Our German audience melted once more back into the city's rubble.

We turned our attention again to our dangerous, deadly, and dirty business at hand.

27
A Child in Distress

It was a bright, cool spring Sunday morning in a small town somewhere in western Germany. Sergeant Dean, my jeep driver, and I were checking over our vehicle that morning. He was filling the gas tank when a young German girl rushed up to me. She was, I guessed, about twelve or thirteen years old. Her hair was strawberry blonde and her skin a clear, creamy complexion. She rushed up to me for help as I was the only officer in sight at the moment.

Between my poor German and her use of sign language, I quickly grasped her problem. She pointed to her left wrist where a slight indentation showed where a wrist watch had been. She explained that she was on her way home from church service when two Russian men had accosted her and stolen her wrist watch. Could I help her find it? Summoning Sergeant Dean we all climbed into the jeep. We drove up and down roads and through nearby woods looking for the two Russians, but to no avail. Because I had more pressing duties, we delivered her to our military police headquarters with the appropriate explanation as to her loss and our unsuccessful assistance.

It so happened that adjacent to this town was a German slave labor camp which our troops had liberated the night before. It must be pointed out exactly how the Nazis operated these slave labor camps. First, the slave laborers were from many ethnic and cultural groups so it would be difficult for these slaves to communicate with each other due to the differences in languages. Also, family members were put into different camps. Living conditions were very poor, since all buildings in a camp were one large bare room like a warehouse. Beds were merely two levels of wooden shelves upon which straw was laid. Men and women were indiscriminately housed in each room. Only two or three small light bulbs hung from the ceiling. Toilets were open stalls at one end of the room. Along one wall was a sheet metal trough with half a dozen cold water spigots. When a slave laborer wished to bathe, that person had to stand naked at the trough and wash. Food was barely enough to keep these slaves alive — about fifteen hundred calories a day. This too was designed to control the inmates as it did not allow them any energy to plot. Each morning all slaves were lined up outside for roll call which consisted of numbers only, since each inmate had his or her number tattooed upon an arm. At the conclusion of roll call, usually one or two numbers were called out and those unfortunate ones were tied to a stake in front of the whole assembly and shot. After roll call, all the slaves were marched to various job sites. All these measures were calculated to de-humanize and control-by-fear the inmates.

These camps were usually controlled by S.S. guards. After repeated "leaks" about these camp conditions, the outside world insisted that the International Red Cross from Switzerland be allowed to enter and interview the prisoners, so this was arranged. One of the features the Nazis told the world was that each camp had a nurse in attendance at the dispensary. Actually, a woman was there about one hour each day, usually in the late afternoon. She was not a trained nurse and the only medicines kept by her were a few bandages and some alcohol for disinfecting wounds. Her real duty was to be a prostitute for the nightly pleasure of the S.S. guards. When the International Red Cross representatives arrived, they found the daily calory count had been increased to two thousand; and a trained nurse was now on duty, and the dispensary filled with an ample supply and assortment of bandages and medicines.

Of course, the International Red Cross representatives insisted upon private interviews with several prisoners chosen at random. These men and women were taken aside and asked whether or not they had enough to eat and how they were treated by the guards. Not one of them dared to complain as they knew the guards knew their identity. If they told the truth, as soon as the I.R.C. representatives left, they would be beaten to death with gun barrels and steel rods.

As soon as the International Red Cross made their reports public, conditions returned to normal in the camps. The whole affair of course was a white wash.

After our troops had freed this slave labor camp, we opened its gates. We de-loused every person and all sleeping areas with DDT. We gave them hearty G.I. rations and promised that as soon as the fighting was over we would see to it that they were sent home. Naturally they were ecstatic!

We discovered that all these measures did not satisfy them; they wanted revenge! Immediately these slave laborers began to sack, really beat-up and rob the German civilians. In some cases they burned down their houses. What to do? We disliked doing it but had to force them back into camp from sun-down to sun-up and stationed a guard at each gate to enforce this order. We simply could not have disorder and violence behind our lines. At the same time, we asked them to volunteer as labor companies to repair roads and railroads in an effort to assist us to win over the Hun. Surprisingly, they did so willingly.

It was two of these slave laborers, in this case Russians, who robbed this young girl that Sunday morning as she came from church.

28
Low Boots and High Water

A separate infantry regiment had driven the Germans back to a river bend after hard fighting. Our Corp Commander had ordered them to secure the inside loop at this point on the river, secure a bridge-head across the river, and build a pontoon bridge so that our Tenth Armored Division could be passed through them. The bridge components were already in the infantry regiment's hands at the proposed bridge site. Higher ranked headquarters had set up a time schedule ordering the infantry regiment to have completed all three of its missions as above by mid-morning.

In viewing these facts, several factors should be taken into account. First, the infantry regiment had been in hard fighting for a month; second, the river was at flood stage and one hundred twenty feet wide, due to the January thaw and was moving from right to left across our zone at six miles per hour. What was normally a sixty foot wide river moving at three miles per hour now was a raging torrent with trees, brush, dead animals, and debris passing downstream. The air temperature was thirty-six degrees F. and the water temperature was only thirty-four degrees F. Skies were overcast with ground visibility fair to poor. The proposed bridge site was at the center of the inside loop. The entire area along both banks was heavily wooded.

Our Tenth Armored Division was approaching the rear of

this infantry regiment on schedule at 1000 hours preparing to cross at the junction. A radio message was received by us from the infantry regiment stating it was receiving so much heavy fire that neither the bridge-head had been established nor was the bridge yet across the river. This delay resulted in stopping our Division in place awaiting the "go ahead" signal from the infantry regiment. Time passed. At 1400 hours our G-3 requested information again about when we could expect to cross over; again the infantry regiment made the same reply. At 1800 hours (now dark) the same request was made and the same answer received.

At 2200 hours, having heard nothing from the infantry regiment, General Morris sent me forward to explore the situation. His explicit instructions were for me to find out the true situation, how much enemy fire was being received, whether the bridging components were indeed at the site, and whether there was any enemy across the river opposite the bridge site.

So off we went into one of the darkest nights of recent memory, Sergeant Dean driving in second gear and both of us straining our eyes to see our way. The little two-track we were trying to follow zig-zagged through the woods heading generally toward the river. Suddenly we were challenged by one of the infantry regiment's out-posts. We stopped and I advanced to be recognized, to exchange the password and the counter-sign. After those little details were cleared, I then asked them how to get to their regiment's command post. They pointed us to the left front, indicating that if we followed the trail of white toilet paper spread on bushes beside the two-track, it would lead us directly to their command post.

We started off again, but this time even slower than before as the night had grown darker and the woods denser, so it took a lot of eye strain even to see the white paper trail markings. After one more challenge, we eventually arrived at their Command Post which consisted of a tent set against a small hill. After going through the two black-out curtains, I found myself inside a twenty foot square army tent. Manning the phone was a sergeant and sitting at a portable desk was a captain, who turned out to be the S-2 of their infantry regiment. The only other item of note inside was a red hot sheet metal stove used to heat the tent.

I presented my credentials asking for permission to reconnoiter the near side of the river bank and to check the bridging as a prelude to our Division's proposed crossing. Such arrangements were routine. The S-2 okayed my request sending me off in the proper direction to reach the bridge site. Actually I took a few extra liberties along the way to the site which consisted of a complete tour of the entire regiment's position. Our time of arrival at the infantry regiment's area was 2400 hours (midnight). Sergeant Dean and I spent the next seven hours on foot roaming the infantry's area and collecting data for our report back to the Tenth Armored Division Headquarters. Due to the flooding of the low area plus extreme darkness, we managed to fall over logs and sleeping men, step into pools of muddy water and skin our shins against bridge sections and boxes of ammunition. During this long dark night, not one round of artillery or mortar shell, nor even a rifle shot came from the enemy's side of the river, so all was totally quiet. The entire regiment was sound asleep including the Colonel in command. We located all the bridge components, most of which had not even been unloaded from trucks. A few of the pontoons for the bridging were unloaded near the actual site and had been inflated ready to be manned and launched the next day across the river.

By 0700 hours our little night's adventure was filled out as to the friendly situation, lack of enemy fire, and the bridging situation. This left one last item on our orders, i.e. were there any enemy across the river? Not having any friendly forces across yet, this problem became more critical. I considered several options. One of the pontoons which were also used as assault rafts could be used to cross over. This idea was discarded because of the six mile per hour river flow which would have required six men to row and we were only two. Without extra men, the raft or pontoon would be difficult to control plus the speeding current would carry us around the elbow of the river into an area where Germans had been reported on both sides of the river as late as yesterday.

A second option then surfaced. I could swim across! This too was discarded due to the low temperature of the river water. Additionally, if I could have safely swam across, coming out of the water "over there" with the air temperature only two degrees warmer would have presented still more problems.

We wracked our heads over this problem. It was still about a half hour until first light. Gradually, the nucleus of an idea germinated in my mind. I informed Sergeant Dean to locate a good safe spot behind a large up-rooted tree trunk and to sit there keeping watch while I knocked the mud from my lieutenant bars. At first light I stepped out upon the river bank and slowly walked back and forth endeavoring to draw fire if there were enemy on the opposite bank. In daylight, I was a perfect target. This may seem a foolish thing for me to do, but after spending all night with no enemy fire arriving in the infantry regiment's area, I was convinced they had pulled back from the far side of the river to a better defensible position. Searching with field glasses across the water at first light, I asked myself what I would do if I were in their shoes. About a mile beyond the river was a low ridge line, a perfect spot for defense. Usually rivers are the best defensive positions possible but this river was in flood stage and all the low areas along the river on both sides were either under water or very muddy. For a good defense, fox holes must be dug. As soon as these would have been dug they would have filled with water. Defensive works dug on that distant hill would be dry. For these two reasons I concluded I was in little danger, but just in case I was hit, Sergeant Dean was to have notified the medics at once.

The "dirty tricks" those Nazis used included their situating sharp-shooters in hollow trees. In searching the woods one could not see them. They would watch through a knot-hole in the tree and when you came into view, they fired their burp guns (rapid fire sub-machine guns) at you. I assumed there were no sharp-shooters across this river, but I could have been "dead wrong".

After parading for twenty minutes and no shots having been fired at me, Sergeant Dean and I retired to our jeep and I sent an encoded message to our G-3 setting forth all pertinent data. You can bet that our Commanding General got on the phone with the infantry regiment Commander and wire connections practically "melted" off the phones. We noticed immediately a vigorous and sudden increase in the infantry regiment's actions. The bridge was completed in record time and our entire Tenth Armored Division crossed over before nightfall that day.

I make no particular claim to fame for what I did. It is told only to illustrate how many of our men and officers used their heads to out-smart the enemy. Few of us were professional soldiers, but as free men we knew how to solve problems. This was our strength. Nevertheless, many paid with their lives while some were wounded, but not one of us ran. We just kept pushing ahead trying to do our best and tried not to think the unthinkable. That was a great tribute to the Tenth Armored Division.

29
Green Salad (Dachau)

For some time, our Army Intelligence Branch (G-2) had been reporting data and terrible stories told by survivors of the Nazi German Concentration Camps. Our Tenth Armored Division's drive toward the Bavarian border with Austria carried us ten miles south and past the German town of Dachau (population: 25,000). This city is located about twenty miles south of Munich. General Morris said to me that he wished to see the Nazi Death Camp located there. As our Seventh Army's Forty Second Infantry Division had just cleared the town and freed the inmates about four hours before that very day, I grabbed my road map and we were off to Dachau.

When we arrived, following the proper army protocol by signing in at the Forty Second Infantry Headquarters, we were furnished a guide. We saw with our own eyes where one regiment of that Division had stacked rifles and became"orderlies" in trying to save and or help the unfortunate inmates. All the stories told about these death camps were absolutely true. We saw two warehouses filled to overflowing, one with shoes of every kind and size from babies' to large men and women's. The other was overflowing with women's dresses, men's and boy's and children's clothing. Both of these warehouses were so filled with items that windows and doors had burst open and the contents cascaded out onto the ground. We also saw the open pits with their iron grates where men and/or women were forced to kneel with hands tied. Then one of the Nazi guards would blow out their brains with a revolver. Those pits and grates were still red with blood from last night's executions. We saw the piles of dead and naked bodies of persons - both sexes and all ages piled like cord wood. We saw the "showers" where no water had ever flowed through the pipes — only poison gas. We also saw the crematorium or ovens. We saw piles of ashes and partially loaded box cars of those ashes. You may wonder what became of those people's ashes. Well I can tell you — their ashes were sent by rail to be used by German truck-garden farmers as fertilizer. Next time you eat a green German salad you may remember this.

But the worst of all were the "living skeletons" who had been starved almost to the point of death. I talked to one of them, a young German Jew who was the same age as as myself (25 years old). He was so weak that he could only shuffle along slowly. He had lost forty percent of his weight and could not stand up straight. He was severely bent over, spoke slowly and intermittently pausing to catch his breath as he confirmed all the above information. My heart bled for him. When one realizes that six million Jews and five and a half million non-Jews lost their lives in this manner, then the enormity of Hitler's "big lie" and inhuman treatment of all people becomes all too apparent. Both General Morris and I returned to our Division that day badly shaken and justifiably greatly angered.

In spite of all that the Forty Second Infantry Division and other agencies could do, most of these "living skeletons" died. We tried to give them our army rations but this only made them nauseous because they were too rich and greasy for their state of health. So the Forty Second went to various town's people and local farmers asking them for milk and eggs to make soft custards which these victims could digest. The Germans said they did not have appropriate food for them - we knew better. Armed search parties were sent out and brought back all the milk and eggs needed. Unfortunately, a day or two had been lost in the process and so most of these survivors passed away due to their previous mis-treatment. Ironically it was observed that on the opposite side of town from the concentration camp, there was a vitamin factory.

So that the German citizens of Dachau would fully understand the terrible thing that had happened in these camps, all were given a conducted tour through them. Most of these Germans knew something about their existence but never viewed them nor admitted any knowledge of their existence. After their "tour", the Dachau Mayor and his wife returned back home and immediately hanged themselves. This certainly speaks volumes about the guilt of the Germans but does not bring back the innocent.

Rumor has it! Yes, the "rumor" was true! When the Forty Second Infantry men first broke open the gates of this concentration camp and realized the horrible situation, they reacted with intense anger against the Nazi guards. The guards, of course, had already thrown down their weapons and surrendered quietly. The Forty Second soldiers began to shoot and beat them with their rifle barrels because they were so enraged. This retaliatory action did not stop until Major General J.J. Collins, their Commanding General, personally stepped between the camp guards and his own troops and ordered them to stop, telling them if they did not, "they would be no better than those bastard Nazi guards". With this direct order and stinging rebuke, his men ceased their attack on the guards.

Inmate of Dachau.

He lost 40% of his body weight.

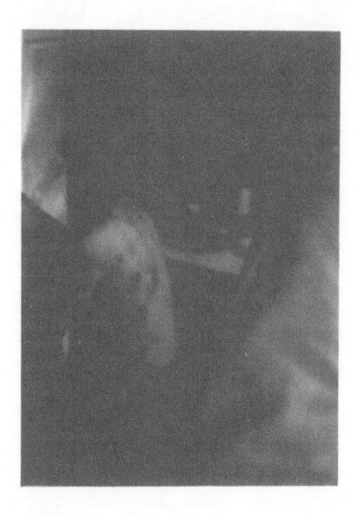

Sores from lice.

30
By Example

The infantry in "Task Force O'Hara" led by Lieutenant Colonel James O'Hara had fought off several counter-attacks one day and had succeeded in driving the German troops back. Late that day, enemy forces had indeed pulled back to a ridge line to "set up shop" and wait for us.

Our men including all officers, were exhausted from this day's battle which had come upon the heels of several previous encounters. The entire infantry contingent, including Lieutenant Colonel O'Hara, had stopped at a grassy tree-covered knoll and laid down in the grass to rest. At about 1400 hours, a message was received from Division Headquarters for this Task Force to take the hill up ahead where the enemy had dug in. The order was specific, "take it before dark".

General Morris, our Division Commanding General, knew full well the German's method of operation as he had been a young captain of infantry during some great battles of World War I. He understood correctly just how tired his men were but he also knew that the hill in front of them was probably not yet heavily defended. During the night, the enemy would surely bring up more troops to secure the hill. If we took it now, our casualties would be light; but if our troops rested and tried to take it tomorrow morning, our casualties would be heavy.

"Smiling Jim" O'Hara slowly rose to his feet and called to his officers and men to form up for the attack. No one moved.

They were just too exhausted. Whereupon the Colonel said "O.K., I guess I'll just have to take that hill by myself", and hefting his M-1 rifle began to walk slowly toward the objective. Later he told me, several thoughts surged through his mind. "What if the men don't follow me?" and "What am I going to do once I arrive all alone at that unfriendly hill?".

He needn't have worried. Almost immediately one of his young infantry men exclaimed, "If the Old Man can do it, I guess I can too." With that exclamation he stood up and joined the Colonel. As if by magic, every officer and man quickly joined them. Together they took the hill before dark with very few casualties.

As predicted, the Nazis tried to take the hill from us the next morning with additional troops. They not only failed, but they took heavy losses for their efforts.

31
Ricochet

At our recent (1991) Tiger Convention in Birmingham, Alabama, E.J. Alexander of Caney, Oklahoma, told an interesting story about what one German artillery shell did to their half-track. He was in Company A Twentieth Armored Infantry Battalion.

T/5 Bill Veltman who was the driver had stopped next to a stone house in a typical rural village. Several rounds of artillery fire began "coming in", so all men took cover immediately. One of these shells hit the side of the stone house about twenty feet above the half-track. When this shell exploded, it shattered the wall sending large stone fragments showering in all directions. One of these wedge shaped fragments was driven into the bogie wheels of the half-track. The vehicle was immovable, i.e., the track could not be moved until the stone wedge could be removed. Besides Alexander, Veltman, Frank Haton and Chuck Kreymire worked several hours in the rain, mud, and shell fire to free that stone from the bogie wheel.

They tried every possibility to try to remove it. To get a good hold on it was difficult as space to reach it was limited. Finally after many attempts, one of the men was able to slip a tire iron under one corner of the stone. With the other three men rocking the half-track by hand, they were able to free the stone from the bogies.

This is just one more example of how intelligent teamwork solved a perplexing problem. That great "can-do" spirit of our Tenth Armored Division came shining through once again.

32
The Barricade

It was inevitable. I knew it should not have happened but it did. Soon we would hit a barricade and this one held a special memory for me. The Germans were good at locating the pinch-points or narrows on a route and then setting up a tank barricade and establishing infantry small arms fire covering it.

Our Division had just been issued new light tanks in exchange for our old light tanks which we eloquently referred to as "buckets of bolts". These new light tanks were almost a carbon copy of our "heavies" in appearance except reduced in over-all size. They had a cast steel turret from which protruded a short barrel seventy-five mm. main gun, the standard co-axial thirty caliber machine gun, and the turret top sported a fifty caliber machine gun for ground and air defense use. They were a three man tank consisting of a driver, gunner-loader, and a tank commander. Before daylight that March day, 1945, General Morris sent me up one of the combat columns to observe an attack. This was not at all unusual but I thought perhaps I should try out one of the two new light tanks which had been recently assigned to the General. So off I went.

The situation up front got a little confusing due to the fact our Combat Command was attacking on two or three parallel roads and cross country. Somehow or other, my tank wound up on one of those parallel roads about a quarter mile ahead of the leading attack tank infantry team. I did not realize my location until I was stopped by a Nazi tank barricade. My driver had buttoned up his hatch and was steering by use of his periscope. As our tank rounded a small bend, the driver saw about two hundred yards ahead of us, a little village. Where this road entered the village was a German tank barricade. The driver stopped our tank, and I rose up out of my turret hatch to have a better look at the barricade. I had just stuck my head out when the turret rang like a bell and I instantly recognized that a sniper was shooting at me. A bullet had hit our tank's turret so I quickly pulled my head in like a turtle.

These new light tanks had a least one improvement which I had not recognized as a good feature until that moment. Someone in our armored development engineering staff really used ingenuity since he had perhaps been in a tank under fire. Below the turret's hatch frame and all around it were three inch thick reinforced glass windows about two inches high and five inches long. One could see three hundred-sixty degrees around the tank without sticking one's head out of an open hatch. To use the tank commander's periscope, one had first to close the hatch. One could see clearly in any direction through these little windows with or without the hatch being closed.

This Nazi barricade was placed between and against two large stone buildings so as to completely block the road into town. Also on my right and at about a forty-five degree angle from the road was a series of farm-village row houses. They had common side walls and one continuous thatched roof. All second floor windows were open on the houses facing us. I removed my forty-five automatic from the holster and placed my tin hat atop it holding it just above the opened hatch. At the same time, I was looking intently through the tank's small windows at those house's open windows trying to see which one held a sniper. Once again he fired and once more our tank turret rang like a bell, but I could not locate his muzzle flash.

I ordered the loader to load three seventy-five mm. H.E. shells and fire them into every other window in the row of houses, beginning with the nearest one to the barricade. I specified every other window because it appeared that each house had one room with two windows. With a seventy-five mm. shell exploding in each house, the explosion would probably kill or wound the sniper, or at least discourage his activities.

After we had fired the three rounds, one of our young infantry officers rushed up and asked me to cease firing as his men were beginning to flush out the row houses and he did not wish to have his men in our direct fire. I readily agreed and informed him of the sniper. Thereupon we backed our tank up a little distance where we could observe our tank-infantry team and still not be in its way. The barricade and row of houses were still clearly in our view.

The tank-infantry team moved rapidly abreast of our tank. The half-tracks moved up another one hundred yards toward the village and they emptied their infantry men out of their rear doors. The assistant gunners fired a few rounds at the house windows as covering fire to allow our men to spread out and go forward. Behind these men, our heavy tanks swung into position in a staggered echelon to the right rear. Their big guns pointed like large "black fingers" at the village. After the half-tracks ceased firing, all was quiet and we could see our men kicking in ground level doors. They fired a few rounds inside, then rushed in to clear out any enemy that might still be present. After this action, they raced upstairs checking out every room on the second floor and in the attic. As each house was cleared, we could see them vaulting walls and entering the next house in the row beyond.

I never did find out whether we had killed or wounded that sniper or simply scared him off. Perhaps he left for a safer area when he saw our tank-infantry men move up. In any event, there was no more sniper fire that day!

It was interesting to observe what happened next. As soon as our infantry had cleared these houses, our engineer's squad began fixing charges to eight upright posts and blowing them off at ground level, thus eliminating another barricade.

This type barricade was typical of several we had encountered. It might best be described as two horizontal sections consisting of ten to twelve inch diameter logs. Each of these sections was held in place by four large vertical logs. Two posts on the left and two posts on the right held the horizontal logs in position. The horizontal logs were stacked between these uprights to a height of approximately eight feet. The uprights were always placed about four feet into the ground and against some sturdy object, such as a stone building on each side of a street. About two feet behind this first log barrier was an identical second one. In between these two barricades, the spaces were filled with large stones and rocks weighing two to three hundred pounds each. Altogether this defensive works constituted an excellent barricade. With enemy sniper fire and infantry fire covering it, none of our men could expose themselves long enough to dismantle it, but we did!

There were several ways to do so. First and most effective, destroy or chase off enemy infantry. Then several options presented themselves. One, was to use two-man saws, axes, and shovels to remove all the trees and/or posts, then using a chain hitched to a truck or tank, haul them away. Also rocks could be pulled out of the way. Such procedures would take about three to four hours to accomplish.

A second technique was to bring up some one hundred twenty mm. guns and blow a barricade apart; resulting pieces could then be removed.

The fastest manner became our third alternative. The engineers would blow the vertical posts and then a tank-dozer would shove all logs and rocks aside. This entire operation could be done in about thirty minutes.

As I watched, in this instance, our engineers blew the horizontal posts. Very soon a tank-dozer quickly cleared the roadway.

We knew that all those trees in this and some other barricades were green with the bark still intact which meant that the enemy had gone into nearby woods, cut and collected large trees and dragged them to the site, erected log barriers and filled in between them with large stones. To erect this barricade, the enemy would need a crane or hoist due to the weight and size of their logs and rocks. This operation would probably take thirty to forty men with horses and trucks about two days. It must have been very discouraging to the enemy to see us tear their barricades down in half an hour.

Much of the great success of our operations was due to our Tenth Armored Division's task force team organization as each had engineers, anti-aircraft, and tank destroyer units. Each of our Combat Command's also had an air corp spotter officer attached to call the Ninth Tactical Air Force if needed. Our present day Army units make much about what they call "integrated forces"; in reality, we were using this same idea a half century ago.

A somewhat similar action took place when we fought up the escarpment (three hundred feet difference in elevation) onto the Swabish Plateau. This high plateau is located in south central Germany. The road up was heavily wooded on both sides, and the defenders had wired charges to trees bordering it. Just as we started, they blew these trees dropping them across our road in a criss-cross fashion effectively blocking our way. Our engineers merely used their chain saws and began to cut down these trees. Tank-dozers then cleared the debris. Consequently we moved forward almost as fast as the enemy could blow trees. This was the first time I knew there was such a thing as a power chain saw.

Barricades did not stop our Tenth Armored Division for very long!

33
Search

This story concerns Nazi possession of much gold with the added luster of American green backs and British Pound Sterling Notes.

Just after our Tenth Armored Division Headquarters settled into quarters at Garmish-Parkenkirchen, Germany immediately after the last days of war, Colonel Wm. Eckles, G-2 of our Division received a phone call. He was called by a German officer who identified himself as Colonel Pfeiffer. He told Colonel Eckles that he (Pfeiffer) understood that Eckles was a trustworthy officer, therefore he wished to surrender to him, but he had a "slight" problem. His difficulty was that he had $100,000 in American "Green Backs" and he knew where $800,000 worth of gold and 5,000 British Five Pound Sterling Notes were buried. Incidentally this money and gold was from the Munich Regional Bank. He would need a couple of GI's and a truck to dig up this "trove" and would then surrender all the money and gold plus himself to Colonel Eckles.

Colonel Eckles thought Pfeiffer full of "hot air" and told him to turn himself in to our American units located nearby in the Innsbruck area and with that Colonel Eckles hung up! He promptly forgot all about the call until the next day when the G-2 of Seventh Army called Bill Eckles stating that they had a "friend" of his there. The Army G-2 said his name is Colonel Pfeiffer, a Nazi S.S. officer. Eckles replied that "he did not know him and he was certainly no friend of his!" Then he related the previous day's phone conversation. At the conclusion of this conversation Colonel Eckles told the Seventh Army G-2 to simply lock him up with other S.S. officers. Eckles felt that the whole story by Pfeiffer was entirely false.

The Seventh Army G-2, however, begged to differ. He explained that the S.S. Colonel had told him the same story and then promptly placed $100,000 in good American money on his desk. He told Eckles that our Tenth Armored Division would have to send a 2-1/2 ton truck and driver, plus an armed guard to Army Headquarters to pick up Colonel Pfeiffer and the $100,000, take him with the money to Austria and there dig up the gold and British Notes, then transport all the cash and gold to S.H.A.E.F. Headquarters. There Colonel Pfeiffer was to be turned over to S.H.A.E.F. P.O.W. Cage. Colonel Eckles could do nothing except comply. A truck, a driver and an armed guard were quickly sent to Army Headquarters and picked up the $100,000 and Pfeiffer and headed straight for Austria.

This was the last anyone ever saw of Colonel Pfeiffer, the money or our truck, driver and guard. For the next five years, our American C.I.A. and its British counterpart, MI-5, combed Europe trying to locate even a trace of them.

Oh! Yes they did finally locate the real Colonel Pfeiffer; he had been in one of our P.O.W. Cages all the while. Supposition was the the bogus Colonel Pfeiffer was a high S.S. Nazi officer in disguise. Investigators deducted that he steered the truck, driver and guard to the area of the buried gold, recovered it, then killed the two Americans, probably disposing of their bodies weighted down in some Alpine lake. He then donned their American uniform, crossed over to Switzerland, deposited his loot in a numbered bank account, sold the uniforms, guns, and truck. He then left for Argentina with forged papers and identification.

To any German today who might read this account and laugh at us, I have some comments which they should consider.

The money and gold from the Munich Regional Bank were stolen outright by a few Nazis for their own use from their own people's bank at a time when southern Germany needed money and gold desperately. The U.S. Government initially furnished funds without interest to establish this Munich Regional Bank - another act of friendship to the German people. Contrast this to the Nazi's theft and one sees a truer picture of the kind of persons the Nazis really were.

Much later, in 1989, Owen McBride, Captain "B" Battery Four Hundred Twenty Third Artillery Battalion, and his wife, Rosemary, along with my wife, Shirley, and I drove over to College Station, Texas for an overnight visit with Colonel Bill Eckles and his wife. We had a wonderful visit and that is when Bill told us this story, thus I have no reason to doubt it. If anyone were acquainted with Colonel Eckles, one could never doubt his word, because no man ever was more upright and honest than our now departed dear friend, Bill Eckles.

34
A-Three Legged Stool

An armored attack has always been characterized by three things: mobility, fire power, and shock action. These are the three legs of our Armored Division's "stool". The first two are readily understandable by most men but the third is more difficult to comprehend.

To clarify this third leg, may I cite one example from our Tenth Armored Division's battles in World War II.

Our Combat Command was fighting the Nazis and as luck would have it, I happened to have been moving forward just behind the lead team. You may recall our Division operated with Task Forces (Battalion) and "Teams" (Companies). The Team I was observing was composed of three tank platoons and three infantry platoons. They had already hammered the enemy badly. As tanks reached about one hundred fifty yards from where the enemy infantry had dug in, our infantry exited out the back of their half-tracks forming a scrimmage line abreast of the tanks and half-tracks. All these vehicles were firing their .30 and .50 caliber machine guns as well as 75 mm. guns at the enemy. All the infantry quickly added its rifle and B.A.R.'s to this attack, as did the artillery.

Rather quickly our line moved forward and overran the enemy's infantry which was still in its fox holes. One enemy platoon in particular was overrun directly in front of me. German members of this platoon were so confused that they stopped shooting and just stood in their fox holes looking at us. Our men ran up to each man ordering him to drop his guns and climb out of his fox hole. The Germans did nothing — just stood there and looked at us and our tanks. Not one Nazi soldier surrendered. Our infantry men again repeated their order. Still the enemy did not move.

At this juncture, our Tank Platoon Commander ordered his heavy tanks to move up to a very short distance from each fox hole and lower their 75 mm. guns directly into the face of each enemy soldier. Again the order was given "to drop your guns and surrender!" This time the order worked but only for those enemy infantrymen into whose face those tank guns were poked. Our tanks and infantry moved on to the next fox hole and then the next. This same procedure had to be repeated for everyone of those enemy soldiers including their lieutenant before they would give up. This psychological phenomenon is termed "shock". To fully understand the situation put yourself in their place. They could have run to the rear but were afraid that we would shoot them once out of their holes, so they remained in place. By then they were in deeper trouble as they had expended their last anti-tank rocket, and all of their 88's had been destroyed by a combination of our artillery, heavy mortar fire, and tank fire. Their artillery was also knocked out by our artillery counter battery fire. All they had left were their rifles and a few hand grenades. They had no idea of surrendering. Where could they go? What could they do now? Most of them were proud of their native land, so to surrender was unthinkable. But here they were in deep travail, torn and traumatized between love of life and fear of death, too proud to give up, yet too realistic not to do so. Their psyche was ripped apart by these overwhelming choices: life or death, surrender or continue fighting in a losing contest.

It was not until our tankers poked their 75 mm. gun muzzles into their faces that these enemy soldiers' minds were made up. I am sure those three inch holes in the gun barrels into which each enemy soldier was forced to gaze that hour probably looked more like two feet. There was no further searching of their minds as to what they had to do now. This was their coup-de-grace, their mortal strike against which all logic and manly pride failed. So they dropped their guns and meekly complied to our command.

It was interesting to observe that none of our infantry shot them while they were in their fox holes. They were ready to do so, of course, had these enemy soldiers shown the slightest indication to fire. In this small section of our front, all firing had actually stopped after our forces overran this enemy platoon. Our men were not blood thirsty, so I gave them much credit. They simply ordered the Krauts to surrender, our tanks moved in, and they surrendered! This illustrates the power of "shock action" that every Armored Division knew so well.

35
A Horse of a Different Color

All the men in our Tenth Armored Division kept a sharp eye out for any cute little filly. I guess it was just human nature with a lively group of young Americans like us.

This is the true story of a cute little filly that caught the practiced eye of Captain Cecil Hill of our Eleventh Tank Battalion.

In the late 1930's, Cecil graduated from the University of Idaho with credentials to teach agriculture in high school but he lacked practice teaching. He also graduated from the senior R.O.T.C. course, and received his Second Lieutenant's bars. As the war in Europe flared up with Hitler's army charging into Poland and the immediate declaration of war by France and England upon Germany, this Second Lieutenant found himself on active duty in the Armed Force training program at Fort Knox, Kentucky. Along the way, he became a First Lieutenant, training raw recruits in Armored Warfare at the Armored Force Replacement Center there. Still later in combat, as a Captain, he served as S-2 of our Eleventh Tank Battalion and also as an adjutant. He landed on Omaha Beach shortly after "D" Day in 1944.

At War's end, the Eleventh Tank Battalion with now Captain Hill found themselves billeted in a small town about half-way between Garmish-Partenkirken and Oberamergau, Germany. It was here that Captain Hill's love for horses led him to a German experimental horse farm where the Nazi's were trying to breed a superior war horse from all of the world's known genetic types. He "appropriated" several of the cavalry horses for our Tenth Armored Division's men to use in recreational riding. In addition, one particular little filly caught his eye. She had not been broken to ride, so he took her for his own, trained her and broke her to ride. He allowed no one else to ride her. He trained her for calf roping, using a German cavalry saddle and German calves. The Germans had never seen a "calf roping" event before and thought he would injure their calves, but this was not so!

About a month after V-E Day, an American Cavalry Colonel asked Cecil Hill if he would be interested in teaching a course in beef cattle production to a class of twenty G.I.'s at the University of Munich. These men would receive two credit hours of University credit, and the course would take three months to complete. Hill agreed to teach the course and left the Eleventh Tank Battalion on detached duty as an instructor. The class was held daily in Munich, Germany so he moved there taking along the young filly. Many of his students and the Colonel enjoyed riding in the Bavarian Hills.

About two thirds of the way through the class, most of his cohorts in the Tenth Armored Division received their orders to go home, since G.I.'s were being sent back to the U.S. on a point system. One received points for length of service, time spent overseas, battles involved in, number of dependents, and medals awarded. Cecil Hill had this option too, but as the Colonel explained to him, he was the only instructor qualified to finish that particular class. So Hill agreed to stay another month longer to finish his assignment.

This extension made his wife back home angry. She felt that their ranch needed his attention. Besides, he had not seen their fifteen month old son as he had been born while Cecil was overseas. To stay one minute longer than required was frustrating to her, but he stayed and completed the course so that his students would receive their credits.

As the time approached for him to leave, he asked the Colonel if it would be possible to take his young horse home with him. The colonel said it might be done, so Cecil Hill proceeded with his filly to the discharge station at Fort Douglas. His orders read "to accompany a horse to the U.S.A.", and was probably the only set of orders issued that way in World War II.

It fell his lot to be shipped home with his horse aboard a French freighter. As he knew little of the French language, he undoubtedly had better communication with his horse than with the ship's crew! The freighter was loaded with silks, perfume, and brandy for trade with the United States. A box stall for the horse was built upon the open deck. Their destination was the New York City Port of Entry.

Just short of the American shore, the ship's captain received a wireless message advising him not to dock at New York as the long-shoremen were on strike. This fact resulted in his freighter going up the Delaware River to dock at Philadelphia. This change was satisfactory except for one fact. This city had no established quarantine port of entry for animals. During the two days the freighter was unloading cargo, Hill could not take his horse off the ship. Frantically he tried to bypass or have someone in authority approve his horse's release. Just before the vessel was to sail back to France, a telegram was received from the Bureau of Animal Husbandry in Washington, which authorized Hill to have a qualified veterinarian check and certify that his horse was healthy.

And so it was that Cecil Hill and his horse boarded a train heading for Salt Lake City, where his wife and her father were to meet them with a horse trailer for the trek back home to Idaho. Actually Hill arrived before his family did and so gave the Station Master a personal check for transportation and feed for his horse, but the check bounced! Hill was understandably upset as he knew that he had sent his wife all of his money during his service. He was able to convince the Station Master to hold his horse until he could secure the cash that afternoon and return to claim it.

On foot, he started off down the street looking for a bank when lo and behold his wife and her father saw him as they drove toward the railroad station. Hill's first words of greeting to his wife were "What have you done with all of our money?". This query resulted in the second time she was angry with him.

When all the details were sorted out, it appeared that she had transferred all of their money to a different bank. She had told him so in a letter which had not yet been delivered to him. All financial obligations were met and so the young filly was secured and the three returned happily back to their ranch in Idaho.

The first time I met Cecil Hill that I can recall was at our Tenth Armored Division Veterans Reunion of 1991 in Birmingham, Alabama. It may have been that we had passed each other many times during the War but neither of us were aware of it. After all, everyone looked alike in those wool olive drab uniforms. When we introduced ourselves, I noticed that he had an injured leg and walked slowly with a cane. He told me that a horse had fallen on him. It seems that the grandson of that cute little filly he brought back from Europe was the horse he was riding in a rodeo in July, 1991. He was on a team engaged in a roping contest wherein two contestants roped a steer by the horns and hind legs, competing against the clock and other contestants. Cecil Hill roped the hind feet of the steer satisfactorily but also inadvertently the front legs of his own horse! Consequently this caused his horse to fall on one of Cecil's legs. The leg was not broken just very badly bruised. By the last day of our Convention, he was able to walk with a soft shoe and without the cane.

To me this exemplified that great spirit of "can do" of our Tenth Armored Division. A man in his late seventies was still competing with twenty-year-olds in a rodeo and often winning Compared to many of the mal-contents of today, he was and is indeed a "horse of a different color".

36
Air Power

During the summer of 1944 we were still stationed at Camp Gordon, Georgia. A discussion arose between Lieutenant Colonel William Beverley who was the Commanding Officer of our Four Hundred Twenty Third Field Artillery Battalion and Lieutenant James Spann who was our Battalion pilot. Lieutenant Spann was an excellent pilot who was later killed in action in Europe.

Spann was about the best military spotter plane pilot I have ever know. He could make his plane do almost anything. One day, he casually remarked to me that he could put a glass full of water on the dash of his plane and do inside loops without spilling a drop. Colonel Beverley overheard him and laughed at his boast, and said he did not believe it could be done. Whereupon, Spann arranged a demonstration flight at the Battalion Air strip next morning with the Colonel and a glass of water.

The two of them took off in the plane with Colonel Beverly holding the water glass so as not to spill it. At the proper altitude, Spann took the glass and placed it upon the dash. Holding the plane at an even keel until the water had quieted, Spann then began his series of inside loops. No water spilled; the glass never moved.

An hour later they landed. Colonel Beverley was so impressed he did not stop talking about this feat for two weeks.

In fact, everyone he met just had to hear this tale, often more than once! I have never seen him that ecstatic before, or since!

Much later during our Division's drive south of Heidelberg, I had to go up in one of our Maytag-Messerschmidt airplanes for airborne observation purposes. The pilot had his plane doing "lazy circles" about two thousand yards altitude and a mile behind our front lines. We were observing various armored columns moving forward and attacking on parallel roads below. Fighting was quite intense so we kept especially alert for the presence of enemy 88 mm. dual purpose guns. There were several but they were much too busy to bother us, since our tanks and artillery were fully occupying their attention. We were still concerned lest they swing their "tubes" upward and fire at us, since we would have surely been "sitting ducks".

All of a sudden the pilot yelled, immediately across our flight path roared a German fighter plane and right behind him, hot on his tail, was one of our pursuit planes. When our little plane hit the back-wash of these two fighters, it was a though we had hit a solid wall.

Our plane dropped like a stone. It was all the pilot could do to regain sufficient air speed to prevent a fatal crash. As it was, he barely leveled out just above the tree tops. After swallowing several times, I managed to relocate my stomach to its original and proper place and so we continued on with our observation mission.

Another event took place that may be of interest. As I recall, this episode took place during our attack and fight to clear the Saar-Mosel Triangle. One morning General Morris had a visitor at our Headquarters, who was the Commanding General of the U.S. Tactical Air Force which was supporting us with fighter bomber strikes. He stated that he would like to see what we were doing on the ground, since he had never had any experience observing ground combat except what he could see from "upstairs" while flying.

With a gleam in his eye, General Morris ordered Captain Smith, our Liaison Officer, to show the General how it's done on the ground by taking him up to the lead Task Force of Combat Command A. No one told our visiting brass that at that very hour Combat Command A was in a terrific fire fight. Several hours later when Captain Smith returned the Air Force General to Division Headquarters, he explained that they had spent several hours crawling in the ditch and mud dodging artillery and 88 mm. fire. After this hands-on-experience, the General vowed that he would see to it that our Division received the best "damn air support" he could provide. He never realized before what "hell" we fought in. He was as good as his word, too! No unit ever gave better air coverage than his Tactical Air Wing provided. From then on one call was all we ever had to make and those "fly boys" came in hard and fast. I often wondered whether he got all the mud off his uniform. We all had a respectful and grateful good laugh at his expense.

Section 2

REFLECTIONS, PONDERINGS AND MUSINGS

37
Armored Artillery

Of all the branches that the infantry and tankers relied most heavily upon and took too much for granted, the Division Artillery stood alone. This may have been an undeserved oversight by them because as we were always there when they needed us.

Several times during the Battle of the Bulge when an especially heavy German Armored attack occurred, they called upon the Artillery to send one or two sections of fire up to help repulse enemy tanks. It is obvious to anyone that our big one hundred five mm. shells pushed by a maximum "charge seven" could do major damage to any Nazi tank up to two thousand yards. If enemy tanks were moving across our field-of-fire, then our big artillery howitzers had difficulty tracking the enemy because our howitzers could only traverse a few mills either side of center before the howitzer M-7 tanks chassis had to be moved. This move was done by starting up their engines in order to move their tubes right or left. If the enemy was coming toward us almost head-on, our gunners scored well and fast. A good Artillery crew could fire one round each second for a short period of time. This is faster than tanks could fire as the maneuvering room inside a tank was crowded and had only one crew man as loader.

I am aware that some of our tanker friends will dispute this evaluation, but as a general rule, it was true. Tanks had two advantages over our open top howitzer. Our armored tanks could fire in a complete circle due to a commutator-type brush delivering power to their turrets, whereas German tanks were limited to 270 degrees as a wire cable delivered power to their turrets. In later enemy tanks this limitation was eliminated.

The second advantage of our tanks was the enclosed armored shield or turret which kept them safe from small arms fire. Our howitzers on the M-7 tank chassis were so constructed that they had a partially armored rim part way around the deck. Up front on the right side was an open top turret having an anti-aircraft ring around its top which mounted a fifty caliber machine gun. These machine guns were used to great advantage against enemy infantry and planes.

Most of the time our artillery was used on "fire missions" meaning indirect firing over the heads of our friendly troops and onto hapless Nazis. Several types of concentrations were used. One of the most effective I believed was the "Time-on-Target" or T-O-T. My introduction to this T-O-T was as a candidate at Officer Candidate School, class 90, at Fort Sill, Oklahoma. Our entire class was taken by truck early one morning out onto the artillery range. The previous afternoon a squad of men had collected some heavy cardboard like appliance boxes. These had been flattened and staked in a two hundred yard square area. We were told to inspect all of this area; we were then transported back to the observation post. Afterwards, a Battalion Time-on-Target of forty-eight rounds was fired. It was timed to explode twenty yards above the cardboard pieces. We were transported once again out to the target area to re-inspect the cardboard. A twenty yards elevation over a target gave maximum destruction effectiveness, we were told.

No place on that cardboard target area of two hundred square yards could one fit a fist between ruptures where shell fragments had punctured. I was impressed. Several times later during combat, the use of Time-on-Target concentrations wiped out entire enemy battalions or regiments of infantry. Later we were issued the "proximity fused shells". These shells automatically exploded fifteen yards from any solid object, i.e. the ground, a building, tanks, etc., thus speeding delivery of shells upon enemy targets as no calculations were required at the artillery fire direction center.

All in all, the Division Artillery did a yoemen's job for our troops. So let's hear it for our artillery lads!

Gen. de Monsabert, Gen. Morris, and Gen. Guillium

38

General William W. Beverley Letters

1.   Copy of letter to his officers and men of the Four Hundred Twenty Third Armored Field Artillery Battalion, dated 9 June, 1984.

MAJOR GENERAL WILLIAM W. BEVERLEY
U.S.A. (RETD.)
310 MANSION DRIVE
ALEXANDRIA, VIRGINIA 22302

9 June 1984

Dear Member of the 423rd,

     July of this year marks my 50th year with the U.S. Government and the U.S. Military. My fondest memories of those past years are the years 1942-1945 that I spent with the very finest group of people. Margaret and I shall always treasure our memories and the friendships we made during a difficult period of our history. Never have I received such complete, wholehearted support during my Army career as I did from you.

     The purpose of this letter is to let you know that our 423rd Armored Field Artillery Battalion Standard (Colors) is still waving proudly. When I left the Battalion at the end of the war, the Division was on orders to return to the U.S. for deactivation. Major General Fay Pritchard, the Division Commanding General, knowing that I was the only Commander of the Battalion, gave the Standard to me to safeguard. This I did until 2 years ago when I presented it to the 10th Armored Division Association for presentation to its museum. I recently discovered that the Association had no museum; so I requested its return to me for presentation to a museum which would <u>display</u> it. This I have done.

     The Commanding General of the U.S. Army Field Artillery Center, Fort Sill, Oklahoma, stated <u>very emphatically</u> that the Center desired our Battalion Standard and would display it in the Field Artillery Museum, which is a very fine museum. Margaret and I flew to Fort Sill. On D-day, 6 June 40th Anniversary, I presented the Battalion Standard to the Chief of Staff of the Center and the Director of the Museum in an Office Ceremony. In addition, I gave them a condensed Battalion history, a roster of key officers and non-commissioned officers, and a large photograph showing Major General Paul Newgarden presenting the Standard to me in 1942.

We were most pleased that our son, whom many of you knew as a toddler, was coincidentally on temporary duty at Fort Sill and attended the ceremony with Margaret. He is a Lieutenant Colonel commanding the 2nd Battalion, 11th Field Artillery in the 25th Infantry Division. *(now a Colonel and is G-3 of Fifth Army in San Antonio).*

Thirty-nine (39) years ago, I wrote the next of kin of each man in the Battalion. Now, I am writing to express to you my heartfelt appreciation for your wonderful assistance and support to me during those difficult days. Margaret joins me in sending our very best regards to each of you.

Sincerely,

William W. Beverley

William W. Beverley
Major General, USA (Ret)

P.S.   Please forgive the form letter, but I am sending it to each member of the Battalion whose address I have. Hopefully, I have not overlooked anyone.

2.   Copy of letter to our Division dated 1 September, 1992.

Major General William W. Beverley
U.S.A. (Retd.)
5203 Bermuda Village
Advance, NC 27006

1 September 1992

Dear Fellow Tigers and Families:

I sincerely regret that I can not be with you to celebrate this 50th Anniversary and do extend my best wishes for a happy get-together. Because of health problems, I am unable to travel.

I have the very fondest memories of my serving with you in the 10th Armored Division. In late June 1942, I reported to General Newgarden and found him with his aide, then Major Sheffield, in a small office in a wooden, old gymnasium. I was the first member to report to the Division. After welcoming me as one of his Battalion Commanders, he told me to look through the division area for a location for my Battalion when the men arrive. I selected General Patton's Corps Hq & Hq Company area - a new wooden complex at the far end of the Division area. When asked by General Newgarden why I selected this area at the furtherest point from the Division Hq, I told him: "Sir, out of sight, out of mind, out of trouble". He laughed and said: "It is yours."

Much has been written or recorded about the tank & infantry battalions, but very little about the three artillery battalions which make up the combined arms team with the tank and infantry units. So here are a few comments relative to the 423rd Armored Field Artillery Battalion. The 423rd Armored Field Artillery Bn, of which I am so proud, was admired by General Newgarden. We produced the first qualified tested Tigers designated as such by the Division. We set the record of 8 hours 1 minute for the 25 mile march after Tiger Camp - there was not a fallout - all the men made the distance as a group. We were declared combat ready after the very first tests administered by the U.S. Armored Forces Hq., and then we furnished personnel to act as umpires to test other units. We enjoyed a fine reputation with all the other units of the Division and also had the Division Champion softball team for three years. Our combat record was outstanding.

When we were on the Tennessee maneuvers, my wife and 2 year old son were in a group of about 30 other wives who camp followed with Mrs. Newgarden. After two (2) weeks of maneuvers, General Newgarden said to me: "Bill, I know you did not leave your battalion area for the weekend until all equipment and men were taken care of, but don't know how you always beat me to the motel. I said: "Sir, I have 2 L-4 airplanes; I can assign one to you". From then on, he flew to the motel area after each week's maneuver and would be sitting outside of his motel, with my son on his lap, waving to me as I arrived.

Although I was only 24 years old as a battalion commander, the youngest in the Army at that time, General Newgarden never showed or indicated any partiality. This I appreciated so very much.

So much for a few memories. Again, I send my best regards and wishes for a very happy occasion to all of you.

Sincerely,

Bill Beverley

39
Able Battery - 423rd A.F.A.Bn.

It was one of those hot summer Sunday afternoons in early July, 1944 at Camp Gordon, Georgia. The sun was beating down unmercifully upon our heads and also sending "heat devils" dancing across the tarmac roads. To escape this heat inside our barracks, I sought out a large shade tree near the Battalion's baseball diamond. It was not only cool but I could also enjoy the afternoon's softball game. The "A" Battery enlisted men were playing a scrub game against the "A" Battery officers. Before the game, I gratefully sat in the shade and breeze while writing a letter home.

The two teams were already warming up and practicing. I had just completed the first paragraph of my letter when Captain Bob Brown walked over to me and drafted me as game umpire. Dutifully I laid down my pen and paper and going out onto the field assumed a proper crouch position behind the catcher. What had started out as a ho-hum quiet afternoon became an exciting one. Both teams were good and well matched.

Soon it was top-of-the-ninth inning. The score was tied two and two. The enlisted mens team was up to bat. They had two outs and one man on third base. I believe the base runner was either Tom Bubin or his buddy Al Jamars. The next pitch came in high and fast. With a loud crack, bat met ball driving it low to the ground just inside the left base line. The left fielder scooped it up on the first bounce, firing it home. Running his heart out, the man on third base slid across home plate just as that ball went splat into the catcher's mitt.

It was a close call but I waved the runner "safe". what confusion! The stands and enlisted mens team went wild throwing their hats into the air, cheering and shouting with joy. At the same time the officers team was certain I had made a bum call since it believed the runner should have been called "out". I was greeted with boo's, whistles and the officers wound up shaking their fingers at me while singing "Three Blind Mice". You can bet for the next two days in Basic Officers' Quarters I was about as popular as that proverbial "Skunk in a Cabbage Patch". My unpopularity soon died out, however, as we had more important things on our collective minds, i.e. the polishing of a winning team for "over there".

On balance, I would have to admit, should one wish to write a letter home under a good shade tree in the hot summer of 1944 at Camp Gordon, it would be much smarter to locate one other than beside our softball diamond for as sure as God made little green apples, Captain Bob Brown would stroll over and "draft" you to umpire his game.

40
Baker Battery - 423rd A.F.A.Bn.

The last field exercise at Camp Gordon before packing for overseas took place in August, 1944. We were in one of those evergreen forests in Georgia. Tree roots tangled above the ground and the terrain was hilly and soil erosion was evident everywhere in rivulets and stream banks.

It seemed reveille sounded earlier that morning than usual. We all rolled out stumbling into line with boots untied, pants not belted and some not even buttoned up. Some had only three buttons on our shirts fastened, and our tin hats slapped over our uncombed hair. The famous yellow Georgia clay clung to our boots and pant cuffs. Our backs were stiff from sleeping on the cold wet ground. As soldiers we can all relate to this scenarios.

All platoon leaders reported to Captain E.O. McBride who was the "B" Battery Commander. When he attempted to about face and report to Colonel Beverley, Battalion Commander, Captain McBride's foot caught in one of those Georgia tree roots causing him to fall flat on his stomach. All of us including Colonel Beverley held our breath trying to keep a straight face. Shaken and embarrassed, our Captain hurriedly stood up.

Suddenly from the rear ranks the oldest draftee exclaimed, "I may be court-marshalled but I can't help it - Haw!-Haw!-Haw!". Whereupon we all roared with laughter including Captain McBride and Colonel Beverley.

It was then I knew I could follow Captain McBride to the ends of earth.   Any man who could laugh at himself was a true leader of men and a very understanding person.   He was my kind of guy.

One day our Four Hundred Twenty Third Armored Field Artillery Battalion was drawn up as part of a Division parade. The entire Division was about ready to "pass-in-review".   Just as the reports to Colonel Beverley were completed by the batteries, Private L— staggered across the parade ground right up to Captain McBride.   He had been A.W.O.L. and was now quite drunk; for this private the episode was all too routine.   He saluted Captain McBride and in a loud voice said: "Private L— reporting for duty, Sir".   The good captain "had had it" with this man's repeated infractions, so turning to one of his sergeants, he directed him to take Private L— to the guard house.

As a result of this episode, two things occurred.   One - Captain McBride was able to ship this man out of his Battery. And second, Colonel Beverley confined Captain McBride to the post for two weeks because the Captain had not been able to control this man's behavior.   Captain McBride always felt that his punishment was unwarranted as this private was an habitual offender and cared nothing about the army or the war.

As a later sequel to this story, Colonel Beverley happened to be sent off to an army meeting which left Major Scott, an Executive Officer of our Battalion, in temporary command. Scott rescinded Captain McBride's confinement-to-post orders. Both officers were well-liked and respected.

41
A Little Night Fishing

On 17 December, 1944 we received our "march orders" to move north in the dark of night to south eastern Luxembourg for the sole purpose of first stopping and then driving in the southern flank of Von Rundstedt's penetration. Each of us can vividly recall where he was and what he was doing when this order came down from Third Army on that fateful day and its subsequent dark night's journey.

As Captain Sam Cohen tells it, that night's adventure reminds him of the "old timer" who heard that night fishing was more productive than day time fishing. So he tried it and discovered this to be true. He was so impressed by his good luck that he marked an "x" on the outside of his boat to locate this exact hot fishing hole for his next night.

Sam was S-2 (Intelligence Officer) in the Headquarters Four Hundred Twenty Third Armored Field Artillery Battalion. Lieutenant Colonel William Beverley, his Battalion Commander, ordered Sam to lead all the Battalion observers (plus two M-7 howitzers for protection) and to travel north to connect up with the rest of his Battalion in southern Luxembourg. Colonel Beverley gave Sam a goose egg (meeting area) of about twenty miles diameter to meet there after daylight the next day. So Sam gathered up his troops and started north.

One of the first unusual things he noted was at a cross

road. The road signs had been turned ninety degrees. Checking his compass, he proceeded forward on the correct road according to his compass and not per the sign post. Enemy agents had a penchant for turning all road signs in Allied areas.

Eventually his column arrived at the outskirts of Luxembourg City. As Sam had no city map of this large city it presented a problem to travel the correct roads to exit on the north-eastern side of town. He saw a bicyclist approaching. He stopped this man and inquired as to the routes. Sam had a little difficulty communicating. Using his poor German and a few words of French plus sign language, Sam finally made his needs clear. Whereupon the cyclist turned his bike around and led Sam's column through the city streets to the correct exit road.

They followed this hard surfaced road for some miles. This road changed into a dirt road and later into a two-track. Still later it disappeared entirely at the edge of a woods. As Sam felt he was traveling in the correct compass course, he ordered the two M-7's forward to lead his column through this woods by pushing over the trees. The rest of the column followed. Coming out of this woods, he discovered a hard surfaced road which seemed to lead in the proper direction.

After traveling up and down many hills and several miles in that dark night, he became concerned as he encountered no American unit. The countryside appeared to be empty. This fact increasingly concerned him. As he approached the next hill, he halted the column. Going forward on foot to the top of this hill, he peered through the darkness ahead. Unable to see any troops, he retraced his steps to his column and told his lieutenant to wait here while he drove forward in his jeep to try to make contact with an American Unit. He further instructed this lieutenant to wait for fifteen minutes. If he did not return by then, the lieutenant must turn the column about retracing their route until some American Unit was found. It began to snow.

Leaving his column by the roadside, Sam drove forward. About ten minutes later, he saw a jeep heading toward him. Stopping this jeep, he inquired if there were any American Units ahead. The other driver replied "yes" and then the other driver promptly turned onto a side road going west.

Having been reassured, Sam drove back to where he had left his column. They were not there! Nor was there any sign that they had ever been there. This was most perplexing. So Sam and his driver wandered up and down this road looking in all directions for his men. Finally they again returned to the spot where he had previously left his column.

From out of the nearby woods came a familiar figure. It was one of his men. He explained that just after Sam had driven forward, an officer of the Four Hundred Twenty Third Armored Field Artillery Battalion walked out of this wooded area and directed their column into it. The entire Battalion was either in the woods or behind it so Sam was unable to see them.

Sam reported to Colonel Beverley who praised him for doing such a fine job of bringing up his column. Captain Cohen thankfully accepted this praise. All the while in his own mind he knew he did not know where he had been, nor where he was now, nor how he had gotten there. Sam's fishing expedition had indeed paid off. Like most night-time fishing ventures he could not have retraced his voyage in this sea of uncertainty. In Sam's own words, "It was one more day that I did not need a laxative".

STATE JOUF

LANSING, MICHIGAN,   MONDAY, DECEMBER 10, 1945

Gen. George Patton Suffers Partial Paralysis in Crash

By JAMES F. KING

MANNHEIM, Dec. 10 (AP) — Nerve specialists were summoned from England and the United States today to treat Gen. George S. Patton lying partly paralyzed from a fractured vertebra in the neck which was broken in an automobile accident yesterday.

An army medical bulletin announced that Patton was completely paralyzed below the level of the fractured third cervical vertebra in the neck and that dislocation of the fourth cervical was being closely observed because of the very serious nature of the injury.

The bulletin said an x-ray showed the fourth cervical had been pushed back in place, however, and that Patton's general condition so far was satisfactory.

He was completely rational, it was explained, and had spent a comfortable night at Heidelberg hospital.

Hurrying to his side by trans-Atlantic plane were his wife and a neuro-surgery specialist, Col. R. G. Spurling of Louisville, Ky. Already at the hospital are Maj. Gen. A. W. Kenner, theater surgeon, and Prof. Hugh Barnes, a British specialist who had been flown from Oxford at the request of Mrs. Patton.

Mrs. Patton was expected to arrive in Paris tomorrow morning and ˙ ˙ ˙ ˙here to Heidelberg either

GEN. GEORGE S. PATTON

42
Battery "C" - 423rd A.F.A.Bn.

There are several stories that are of interest concerning the personnel of this particular Battery "C". At one point during our breakthrough of the Siegfried Line, this Battery was firing furiously at enemy lines ahead. Tactically, our Tenth Armored Division was ordered to attack through the Sixty Fifth Infantry Division and to take the city of St. Wendel, Germany on 15 March, 1945. Directly behind our "C" Battery, some eight hundred yards, was a field artillery battery of the Sixty Fifth Infantry Division. This Battery was properly firing over our heads.

Sergeant F.J. Hamner was a Section Chief in "C" Battery. As he relates the story, he was sitting on one of the cannoneer's seats atop his one hundred five mm. howitzer carriage. All of One Hundred Five Armored Field Artillery howitzers were mounted on M-7 tank carriages. On the right front corner of each was what was referred to as "a fixed turret which was armored on all sides but open on top". On the top of this round turret was a ring mounted fifty caliber machine gun. This weapon doubled as close-in defense for each howitzer piece as well as having anti-aircraft capabilities.

On this particular night, Sergeant Hamner was directing his howitzer's firing as usual. All of a sudden several enemy 88's opened up, firing directly at them. Fortunately for the "C" men, the enemy's fire sailed just over their heads and hit the Sixty

Fifth Infantry Division Unit behind them.   F.J. said he did not know whether he was scared or not, all he could recall was that his knees were knocking together so violently that he had to reach down and hold his legs still.   Luckily none of those 88 rounds hit "C" Battery personnel.

At one point later during a night advance, the Sergeant's howitzer slid off a slippery road, turning upside down in a narrow cut and pinned one of his cannoneers inside the front round turret which had been driven into the hard earth. Hamner could hear his man call for help from inside the trapped enclosure. As it was dark and no lights were allowed, F.J. and the rest of his crew had successfully jumped off just as their howitzer carriage was rolling.   They located some pioneer equipment (shovels and picks) and began digging their trapped buddy out by burrowing under the turret to allow him an escape route.   They worked speedily as everyone was concerned that the carriage would burst into flames.   As it did not, the cannoneer soon was released.

It was then determined that their carriage could not be salvaged nor lifted free from its upside-down position.   There was neither a wrecker nor a crane large enough to do this short of "Com.-Z" rear so in order to deny the enemy any salvage that might be recoverable, a magnesium explosive was set off at the bottom of the carriage adjacent to the fuel tank.   The ensuing flames lit the night sky accompanied by an explosion of the few rounds till aboard.

Another event of interest also took place in "C" Battery. Private Dean O. Plimmer was enticed by one of those small decorated stoves which many German houses used to heat a room. He made a deal and purchased one from a housefrau. He had no sooner loaded it into their half-track than the Lieutenant Glenn E. (Cab) Callaway gave the order to mount up and prepare to move out.

At this juncture, the housefrau ran out of her house making a terrible fuss and waving her arms and shouting. Lieutenant Callaway finally figured out that she felt that Plimmer had cheated her in the purchase of that stove by paying too little. Lieutenant Callaway simply looked at Plimmer and told him to give her five more Invasion Marks. This silenced her so the column moved out with Plimmer, stove and all.

Still a different story about "C" Battery concerned a "red" quilt. It seems one of their men decided that his bed roll needed some additional warmth. So he "liberated" a red quilt from a German house. This housefrau complained to "C" Battery officers who then questioned their men. No one knew anything about the "red" quilt. Later, one of the "C" men admitted sitting on it in his half-track even as Lieutenant Callaway queried him about it.

43
The Night the Cannoneer Wept

It was one of those terribly frigid cold nights in December, 1944 during the Battle of the Bulge. Sergeant F.H. Hamner was one of the howitzer section chiefs for "C" Battery of our Four Hundred Twenty Third Armored Infantry Battalion. He related this story to me later.

The Sergeant and his cannoneers had settled down for the night and "forty winks". He and his gunner were sleeping in their bed rolls on top of the howitzer's deck which was mounted on a M-7 tank chassis.

The rest of Sergeant Hamner's howitzer crew had to sleep on the ground. They scooped out trenches wide enough for three men to sleep abreast. They laid down some pine branches over which a tarp was then placed. Next came their three bed rolls and on top of all of this was another tarp to prevent heavy weather from penetrating. These men also piled up snow which had been scooped out of their trench on the windward side to act as a wind break. All these efforts were to conserve body warmth.

This particular night, fog developed as usual about 0100 hours. With no wind to dispel it, this dense fog usually lasted until 0100 to 1100 hours the next day. The fog was so dense one could not see more than ten feet day or night, and invariably, fog penetrated and froze the marrow in one's bones. It was bitter cold that night.

Sometime after Sergeant Hamner had fallen asleep, he was awakened by someone softly weeping. Because of the dark and fog, he could not see who it was that was crying. He kept looking over the side of his howitzer platform trying to penetrate the fog and darkness. Out of the mist, he could make out a man slowly crawling on his hands and knees toward his howitzer. As there had been no recent incoming enemy fire, he was puzzled why this man was weeping.

When this G.I. got close enough, Sergeant Hamner reached down, grabbed the man by the collar, and pulled him up over the side of his howitzer and onto the deck. Here he questioned him as to why he was weeping. It seemed that this G.I. had crawled into his bed roll with his boots still tied on his feet.

This is one of those things no one was to do as it cut off blood circulation in the feet. As one sleeps, feet freeze, so every man and officer had been instructed to untie and remove his boots, and stick them down inside the bed roll while he was asleep. Such a procedure would not only prevent frozen/frost bitten feet, but also kept boots fairly warm and dry and comfortable when worn again. Obviously if boots were muddy or dirty, one simply knocked off the mud or dirt prior to inserting the boots into a bed roll. While this man may have been too tired to observe these simple precautions, he certainly learned a dear lesson.

Having discovered what was wrong, Sergeant Hamner quickly cut the man's boot laces and removed his boots. Then he slid this hurting cannoneer into his own bed roll beside him. Sergeant Hamner's body warmth gradually thawed the cannoneer's feet; this probably prevented the later amputation of his toes. Anyone who has ever had frost bitten toes knows that they are sensitive to cold for many days afterwards. This man's toes were also sensitive, and so Sergeant Hamner saw to it that he had duty which kept his feet out of the snow and off the cold ground insofar as possible.

So this is the true story of the weeping cannoneer.

Luxembourg

| Col. Eckles | Crown Prince Felix | Major Gen. Morris | Maj. Gen. Gay | Brig. Gen Piborn |

44
Shadows of the Mind

In any segment of life's journey, there is always laughter as well as tears. I would like to share with you some bits of humor that helped us keep our sanity in those trying times.

After I had been through a lot of combat situations with my jeep driver, he felt that he knew me well enough to confide in me a little joke that the enlisted men were passing around at Division Headquarters about General Morris and me. General Morris was slightly over six feet tall and I was only five foot seven inches if I stretched! We were privately referred to as the "Mutt and Jeff" of Division Headquarters. This label was too good to keep and I told Colonel Thayer, our Chief of Staff, who had a good laugh too. I never told the General but I always suspected the Colonel told him as they were very good friends.

General Morris told me one time that he had been a cigarette chain smoker. One day when he was in Command Staff College and taking a map examination, the constant fidgeting with those weeds and matches exasperated him. He threw them on the floor and stepped on them. He never smoked again but I many times noticed he <u>did</u> chew gum. His jeep driver told me that he could tell at a glance what kind of day was afoot. If the General climbed into the jeep and was passively working the gum, it was going to be a good day. But if his eyes had a glint and his gum was taking a beating, someone was going to "catch hell", before the day ended.

45
Keys

Under the heading of "leadership", many stories can be related quite truthfully. Some are even amusing - one that especially delights me concerns some "keys" the Germans lost. This incident was reported through our Division G-2 channels just about the time, in early 1945, we were striving to cross the Saar River and punch through the German West Wall or Siegfried Line, as we called it.

In June, 1940 after the British had been driven out of Dunkirk by Nazi Panzers, the German High Command saw little reason to maintain troops in their "Siegfried Line" which ran along their French-Belgium borders. This defensive line of tank traps and camouflaged pill-boxes had been hastily but skillfully constructed in 1939 after the Allies had declared war on Hitler for his invasion of Poland. Had the Allies attacked in early 1939 they could have entered Germany because this defensive line had not been built and because the Allies had many more divisions of troops than Hitler. With the usual German efficiency, these deficiencies were eliminated by late 1939 or early 1940.

After Dunkirk, the Germans closed their west wall. Each pill-box had its own lock and key and so all pill-boxes were locked and all keys given to one officer for safe-keeping. As the war progressed, somehow this officer was shipped to the Russian front where he died in battle.

In 1944 when we landed in France and had fought our way toward the Fatherland, the German High Command became concerned and so ordered their west wall to be opened and staffed with a few second-rate troops. They believed that their first-line troops could fall back and fill up these defenses if need be. In the meantime, defenses would be ready and partially staffed.

To their consternation it was then they discovered that the officer charged to keep these keys was dead and no one knew their where-abouts. The Germans were literally locked out of their own defense system.

What to do? They did the only logical thing possible. They rounded up all the locksmiths in western Germany to pick those locks and make new keys. Shortly after, they re-entered their own pill-boxes.

This true story always amused me to think that those super-efficient Prussian Generals were outsmarted by their own stupidity.

This story of the "lost keys" came to our attention after we had broken through the Siegfried Line and interrogated captured German troops. This action was in January 1945 or about two months after we first hit the switch position of the Siegfried Line.

46
Road Block

This story of General Morris was told to me in 1945 by Lieutenant Colonel McChristian (now Major General). At that time Colonel McChristian was Chief of Staff of our Division. It seems one time General Morris had gone forward to check on the progress of his lead task forces. Lieutenant Colonel Cherry had reported that his Task Force was held up by a road block, a mine field, and heavy small arms fire. General Morris crawled up to the road block with Colonel Cherry and putting his hand on the barrier he turned to Cherry and said, "If I can put my hand on this obstacle then you can certainly find a way over, around or through it". He did just that post haste.

This story is one I had not heard before as I was not present, since the General had sent me to the other column that day.

47
The Palatinate

The dictionary defines the "Palatinate" as an area west of the Rhine River and administered by Bavaria. It was an area of small rural villages. Very early one morning Colonel Sheffield, our Division G-3, asked me to locate a building into which he could move our Division Headquarters that noon. As I had been ordered by General Morris to go forward to one of our combat command columns for observation, and since Colonel Sheffield knew this, I readily agreed. By 1100 hours, after diligently searching through all those small villages ahead on our line of attack plus several villages which were short distances right or left of that direction, I settled on the most likely building. It was a local school house but very different from those back home.

This building had several merits in its favor. It was large enough to house our Forward Command Post and its walls of solid stone were fourteen inches thick. All its windows were narrow and high allowing daylight to enter and also giving protection from shrapnel. This really was the only building of any size in all those small rural towns. Accordingly, I sent coordinates, properly encoded, of this building to the Colonel. Thereafter, I took off on my duties as observer as an extra pair of eyes and ears for General Morris.

About 2100 hours that same night after logging many miles criss-crossing forward areas through mud and incoming fire, Sergeant Dean, my jeep driver, and I returned to this schoolhouse into which our Division Headquarters had moved that afternoon. We were bone tired and hungry. So after reporting to the General, we heated up a "C" ration and using some liberated German bread, settled down to a good hot meal.

Speaking of meals, the Germans had an interesting way to feed their troops. Every third day a portable oven was hauled into a village behind their lines. A baker then mixed up dough and baked two to three hundred loaves of bread. Rumor had it that this bread was a mixture of dark molasses, rye flour, yeast, and finely ground pine chips. The bread certainly smelled and tasted like pine forest, dank and sour, but not unpleasantly so. It also was very heavy and had tough crust and chewy texture. After those loaves had cooled, they were then piled like cordwood unwrapped against the inside wall of a public building. Here, a German soldier would file past, each man taking a loaf and filling his wine bottle from a keg of wine provided. He then placed the bread and bottle into his haversack. This ration had to last him three days before a new supply would be furnished to his unit. He could eat it all in two days but would then go hungry the third day - this was his option!

After downing my heated "C" ration and a chunk of German bread, I went upstairs to the main floor where several men and officers had sacked out in their bed rolls on the floor. (All furniture had been removed from this room and all windows in the building had black-out coverings.)

Being tired, I immediately went into a deep sleep. Suddenly I was awakened by explosions just outside the building. It seemed that a truck loaded with five gallon cans of gasoline had been hit by enemy artillery fire. This truck and an

American ammo truck had just arrived in the parking area beside our Headquarters. As luck would have it, the ammo truck driver cranked up and headed down the street away from Division Headquarters but the fuel truck exploded in a fiery roar, sending blazing and exploding five gallon cans skyward. Some of them fell upon a row of farm houses igniting their thatched roofs. Fortunately our building did not burn as it as solid stone with a heavy slate roof. No one to my knowledge was hurt or killed from this barrage.

When some of the burning five gallon gasoline cans landed upon those thatched roofs, the village fire alarm sounded and the entire village of about seventy old men and women of all ages came running into the streets. Immediately they formed a human chain continually passing buckets of water taken from the town's one and only central fountain down the street, and up ladders to other villagers already on the burning thatched roofs. These buckets of water were then thrown on the fire, and the empties returned for re-filling. It wasn't long before the town fountain's water supply was depleted. Automatically, people began to fill their empty buckets at sump pumps located in nearby manure piles. Thus without losing a moment's time they had switched to the only other source of water available. Eventually all roof fires were exterminated and then all citizens returned to their beds. During this time, some of our men had a few chuckles over this village's antiquated fire system, but it worked!

Next day and for several weeks thereafter, whenever the sun warmed those "saved" roofs, there must have been a "unique perfume" wafting through these houses and their environs.

The real hero that night was the ammo truck driver who moved his truck as the first shells arrived and drove his load of high explosives out of town and harm's way. His doing so avoided a potentially deadly explosive situation and at the same time he risked his life to save others. Such was the spirit once again of our great Tenth Armored Division.

If you have ever been awakened suddenly from a deep sleep, then you can relate to my experience that night. My first groggy thoughts, due to the intense heat and orange light coming through the blacked-out windows, was that I surely must have died and gone to hell. Then I realized that I was still in the same room where I had gone to sleep. Besides, I was now all alone and had I actually descended into the Devil's lair I would have been surrounded by many friends and fellow soldiers. Quickly I saw the situation and immediately grabbed my boots and ran down the hall (past those loaves of German bread still stacked like cord wood) to the basement. Here I met all the other blurry-eyed officers and enlisted men of our Division's Headquarters. Some were lying on the floor trying to sleep once more. Others sat on the floor leaning against the walls. In one corner our Division's telephone switchboard was manned and operational. None of its lines were out. At the switchboard, I first learned exactly what was happening outside.

Colonel Sheffield walked over to me and in his usually diplomatic way said, "How the hell did you pick out this blank - blank building for our Division's Headquarters to move into?" Seizing my self-control with both hands, I calmly replied, "This was the only building large enough in the entire area. I personally checked some eight villages and there were no others except churches and you know it is against Army policy to put combat units in them as this would not comply with the Geneva Convention's provisions; and you know also our Army lives and dies by that agreement." At that Colonel Sheffield walked away. I did notice later that he never again asked me to locate a building for our Division Headquarters.

This story does not end here until I add another dimension. This little town we were in that night was exactly like every other rural village throughout Europe's bread basket area. It made little difference whether a rural village was located in France, Belgium, Germany, or Poland. In each village, houses were separated by common walls. Also, overhead each series of row houses had a common thatched roof. On the lower floor cattle and farm animals were kept at night. The family slept and lived on the second floor while the third floor or attic under the sloping roofs were used to store grains, hay, and buckets of eggs in "water glass". Out front of each first floor's barn door was a manure pile. These dung piles had their own enclosure made of stone walls about four feet high on all sides. The bottom was cemented and sloped to one corner. Above the enclosure's sump, was a pipe leading upward to the top of the wall where a pitcher pump was located.

All human "night soil" as well as cattle dung was tossed each day upon this dung heap. Following this procedure, a ritual took place when each farmer threw several buckets of water onto the manure pile. All this liquid then slowly percolated downward ending in the sump. Periodically, the farmer would bring up his "honey" wagon to his sump and pitcher pump. This wagon consisted of a long oval shaped wooden tank with a removable bung on top and a wooden spigot at is lower rear. This tank would probably hold two to three hundred gallons of liquid fertilizer. The wagon had wide wooden wheels and was drawn by a team of horses or oxen. Pumping out the contents of the manure pile's sump by means of a pitcher pump, resulted in a thick dark brown highly odorous liquid fertilizer which was poured into the tank via the top bung. Driving out into his fields, the farmer cracked the spigot allowing this liquid to drip or drizzle between the rows of his crops.

Ayl, Germany

General Walker	General Morris	Lt. Chapman
Twenty Corp. Commander	10th Armored Div. Commander	10th Armored Division

48
Patton

Every now and then during life's journey a particular incident stands out in one's mind. One "clearly rings a bell" in my memory even after all these years.

General Morris and I had gone forward early one morning to check the progress of one of our lead teams. It had been ordered to cross a small stream and drive the Huns from the opposite bank and establish a bridge-head. Once the bridge-head was established, a pontoon bridge was to be put in for tank and wheeled vehicles. The name of this stream escapes me, but as I recall it was a fairly small one.

When we arrived just at first daylight, the battle had been joined with small arms fire and mortars. Both sides were firing across the stream at each other. The General and I climbed out of our jeep jumping into a shallow ditch beside the road so we could see the action better and also to converse with the Infantry Team Commander. This location also afforded us some protection from direct fire across the river.

Just a few minutes afterwards, a familiar sound echoed over the hills. It was the air horn on General Patton's jeep. His driver drove boldly up to our location in plain view of the enemy. The jeep was all spit and polish as usual with its red bar and four gold stars prominently displayed above the front bumper. Patton calmly got out, motioned to us and, turning his back on the enemy, deliberately spread an aerial map on the hood of his vehicle. General Morris, the Infantry Captain and I had no choice but to join him standing around the hood of his jeep.

At this point, I could almost feel the enemy rifle bullets piercing my back. But miracle of miracles! The Germans stopped firing. It must have been that their commander ordered the cessation. The battlefield near us became deathly quiet. Patton gave Morris his instructions and then calmly drove away. As soon as he disappeared, the three of us hit the ditch; immediately firing began again.

The only sense I could make out of this halting of German fire was to assume that we were fighting a German regular Wehrmacht army unit and not the S.S. troops. Many regular German officers held Patton in high respect as well they might. They never knew when or where he would attack next and when he did, his forces usually made a breakthrough, delivering a severe blow to the Germans. As professionals, they regarded him with great respect.

Had they been S.S. troops, we would all have been surely dead. In truth, most N.C.O.'s and officers of our Division felt as I did about the S.S. In our .45 automatics we saved the last round for ourselves. No one would capture us if we could humanly avoid it. The S.S. had a nasty habit of disarming all prisoners, then marching them into a nearby woods where they shoot every one with machine gun fire. The only soldiers not immediately killed were those who had special information who were first tortured and then shot, i.e. they never captured and retained prisoners. So indeed we were fortunate that morning to have been fighting the "regulars".

For many years there had been a running argument

among many as to whether General Hodges (First Army Commander) or General Patton (Third Army Commander) was the better leader. In General Bradley's autobiography he states that General Hodges was better overall than Patton. I cannot agree with him! Patton drove forward daily to every section of the front and knew exactly where and what his Third Army was doing. By stressing attack rather than defense, all Third Army men and officers were kept alerted. Hodges seldom went forward of his Division's Headquarters and so really did not know the front on a personal basis. Hodges operated like most generals by sending someone else to determine the situation and report back — not so with Patton!

Actually there are two different modes of operation which these two generals exemplified. The first carried the idea that an army commanding general was the product of a long and costly training program. Logically then that country's investment in him should be protected by requiring him to go no further forward than his Division's Headquarters. This, of course, was General Hodges' mode as well as all the other Army Commanders on the Western Front.

Patton on the other hand illustrated the opposite view that a commanding general and all officers must be forward with their men so they could see for themselves what the enemy was doing and how their troops were fighting and noting any supply shortages. Patton's idea was a "hands on" or personal approach. He cared little or nothing about his own well being so he was at the front daily from 0600 to 1200 hours. Also by being well forward, General Patton could make instant adjustments of his units.

Our armies were not the only ones whose Commanding
Generals followed one or the other of these approaches. The
German generals did likewise. Those who operated like Patton
up front with their troops included several of their top generals,
i.e. Rommel and Von Monteuffel.

General Bradley claims[4] that Hodge's army moved faster
than Patton's once we all began to charge toward the Rhine
River. In rebuttal, may I point out two facts that Bradley
appears to have glossed over. First, it was the Tenth Armored
Division that seized the Romer Bridge over the Mosel River and
captured Trier. The city of Trier was the southern anchor of the
entire German defensive line. Our action turned the left flank
of their defenses and forced the pullout of their entire front. Our
Division was the point of Patton's Third Army and this action
followed tremendous fighting to obtain capture of that bridge.

True, all Allied Armies put great pressure along the
German front but none had a breakthrough except Patton's
Third Army. As the Nazi's began to pull back from their
defensive positions, our Air Corp. Infantry and Armored
Divisions pounded them so hard they could not develop a stand
on this side of the Rhine River. As always, General Patton
"broke the dam" which caused a flood of military might. Part of
this flood which followed, was Hodges' First Army leaping
forward toward the Rhine. It is possible that the First Army did
go more miles per day for a very short while, but Patton's Army
did the spade work making this offensive possible.

It should be further pointed out that Patton's Army was
many miles more distant from the American supply ports than
was the First Army's. Patton needed more gasoline due to a

---

[4] Autobiography by General Omar Bradley

preponderance of armor hence his supply was rationed which then slowed his advance.

It has been recorded that at one time when General Eisenhower met Patton during the Battle of the Bulge, Ike winked at Patton and said, "Georgie, why is it that every time we meet I give you an additional star?" Patton replied abruptly, "Could it be because I keep pulling your chestnuts out of the fire?".

Those of us in Armored Divisions who served under General Patton were blessed by a man who knew armor and how and when to fight. He was likewise very good with infantry and artillery. In short, he exercised a sixth sense of timing and expertise that no other Allied General could demonstrate. As evidence of this conclusion, he was the only Army Commander of whom the Germans were afraid. They had a Colonel whose only job was to keep tabs on Patton. No other officer in the Allied ranks was so "distinguished".

In my view, had General Hodges gone forward daily to visit his leading platoons and companies, he would have known that there were gaps within and between units of his front line troops, but he did not. Unfortunately, across the line from him was General Von Monteuffel who roamed the front daily and continuously. It was this German General who discovered these gaps within Hodge's First Army. He made good use of this knowledge when it came time to begin Battle of the Bulge by sending his Fifth Panzer Army through these gaps.

This action never could have happened with Patton's Third Army. Should Patton have discovered any gaps, he would have filled them then and there; heads would have rolled as well. With Patton, every fact was known, weighed, and then acted upon quickly. So my vote goes to Patton as opposed to General Bradley's choice.

As soon as our Tenth Armored Division had pushed north into Von Rundstedt's flank, Third Army ordered its supply personnel to move their six supply dumps northward to an area just south of Luxembourg City. This relocation would support Patton's attack against the German saliest. In just seventy-two hours all six dumps were moved north ninety miles over crowning blacktop roads slick with ice and snow and through fog and dark of night. The tonnage so moved was 174,000 tons. This has to be a record! One more reason I vote for Patton!

Lieutenant Chapman

General George Patton   General William Morris   General Walton Walker
U.S. Third Army Commander   Tenth Armored Div. Commander   Twenty Corp Commander

49
Barger and Lodzinski

"Barger and Lodzinski" sounds like a vaudeville team — right? Wrong! These were the last names of two very fine young Sergeants in our Division's Headquarters. Andy Lodzinski worked for the Chief of Staff, and Ralph Barger for General Morris. Their expertise was that they could type one hundred five words per minute and take rapid dictation, so they served as private secretaries for those two officers. Most persons do not realize just how much paperwork is required in a Division. Like most large corporations, it leaves a paper trail.

It was about the time (1944) we cleared the Saar-Mosel Triangle that General Morris asked me to obtain and keep up-to-date a set of aerial maps of the area of our Division's front. He wanted to have it stream and ridge lined. Because I had gone forward so much, I asked these two Sergeants to obtain maps and stream and ridge line them, after which they were to nail them to the wall of the General's office for his use. As neither of these men knew how to stream and ridge line maps, I taught them. From that day forward, the General had his maps for sure!

At first, I did not comprehend why the General would stand studying them so intently, but I never asked. Suddenly it dawned upon me — he was checking out all possible routes we could take in attacking the enemy. Also he checked their routes to attack us. This review included all the possible "pinch points", i.e. defiles, high ground, assemble areas that would be in defilade — both their and ours, roads and railroads, bridges and any small streams which could channel our Task Forces.

To demonstrate how well he retained data, I will relate an incident. The General and I were in his jeep going forward to a Task Force. With a map in my hand, I instructed the driver to turn right onto a small trail, whereupon the General immediately stopped us, informing me that this small trail was not the correct one. "We should take the next trail to the right", he stated. Even without a map in front of him, he was indeed correct. My error!

After the war was over, Sergeant Lodzinski returned home to Muskegon, Michigan where he worked at Bennett Pump Company in charge of its quality control. The Bennett Company manufactures gasoline pumps and service station equipment, and has done so since about 1900. As I recall, Andy died of heart failure in the early 1980's.

Unfortunately, Ralph Barger had a different experience. One day near Kaiserlauten, Germany, our Forward Division Headquarters moved into a different town and so cleared out an old school house to set up the Headquarters. As usual all the furniture in the building was moved out onto a dump pile. Then the building was swept clean, black-out curtains installed, communications set up, both radio and phone, and our "war room" established. This war room was the nerve center of our Division's activities. On one wall was maintained a large map of our area, including up-to-the minute locations on all our units, mine fields, and forward supply dumps. It also included all known data as to enemy location, etc.

I arrived back at Division Headquarters about 1400 hours that same day just in time to see medics load Sergeant Barger into an ambulance. It seems that as they were cleaning out that school building, someone found a live German (potato masher) grenade. Instead of calling the ordinance boys to come and destroy it, this man simply laid it on the pile of junk out back. When Sergeant Barger had finished sweeping up, he carried the debris out to this junk pile and threw it on setting off the grenade and sending shrapnel through his knee. When I discovered the true facts, I was so angry that I could spit fire. Here was a very fine, healthy, American injured by one of our own men's careless acts. Barger's knee would be forever stiff and painful. I was so mad that had I found the man who did this I could have throttled him with my bare hands.

This was the last time I ever saw Sergeant Barger and for the rest of the war Sergeant Lodzinski had to do double duty as there were no replacements for Sergeant Barger. Many times since the war, I have tried to locate Sergeant Ralph Barger, but to no avail. I just wanted to shake his hand and tell him how sorry I was about his accidental injuries. I tried to locate him through the Army as well as through Veteran's Administration Hospitals. It seems that after World War II all these records had been shipped to the Army Record Storage unit in Kansas City. Shortly thereafter, a fire destroyed most of them. If anyone reading this story can tell me of the whereabouts of Sergeant Barger, I would be most appreciative.

50
Counterpoint

In the long course of world wars until the May-June 1940 Blitzkrieg by German Generals Guderian and Rommel, the world's military officers held that the infantry was the queen of the battle. When infantry was combined with artillery, it could readily take and hold ground. Tanks were considered little more than undependable cavalry, since they become disabled frequently in the early days and thus they were considered of little value. It was heard from many quarters that the only possible use of tanks was to throw them into battle at the proper moment to assist the infantry's efforts. Therefore, tanks were often situated behind infantry units for this purpose. Almost no one considered using them as an independent force of armor nor as a separate armored division until that fateful day, 20 May, 1940. The limited use of tanks was the number one mistake.

Both communications and tactics strategies were completely redefined by this German Blitzkrieg. The British Army did have voice radios by 1939 but its orders were to leave their radios back in England when the British Expeditionary Force sailed for France to join French and Belgium troops. Soldiers were told that France and Belgium had good telephone and telegraph lines so that radios were not required. Wire lines had been adequate in 1914 - 1918 and still were thought to be. This was mistake number two.

The third mistake was the limited use of motorized

transportation. Horses had been found useful over the centuries as beasts of burden. The European rail systems were excellent. Using horse drawn wagons from the many rail heads in Europe made good sense at one time. Motor transportation was relatively scarce, expensive and fuel difficult to obtain. This fact was especially true of German transportation during its Blitz. It has been claimed by Len Deighton in his book <u>Blitzkrieg</u> that the German Army was hampered by lack of motor vehicles and fuel until after France capitulated in June, 1940. At that time it collected all trucks, tanks, guns, armored cars, and fuel and ammunition from its defeated Allied Armies. Before this time, German industries could not keep up with the Nazi Army's demands for transport and fuel.

One of the perplexing problems of tactical warfare before 1940 was the most effective limits of penetration into enemy lines. It was argued with considerable proof from combat situations that the depth of penetration could not exceed one-half the base. This meant that if a division held a two mile front, that unit should not exceed one mile's penetration into enemy lines. To disregard this rule would result in disaster to the attacking division as the slope of its lines would create a bulge of sufficient angle and length to invite a counter attack. The counter attack on each flank of the bulge would cut off the point of the penetration causing disastrous loss to the attacking force.

In several books written about World War I, it has been pointed out that this was what actually did happen to a German salient near the close of that War. The French and English armies cut off its overly extended penetration and the Germans lost 100,000 men. This loss effectively put a crimp to Germany's future military activities as it was running short of manpower.

Our own Army fully subscribed to this thinking until 1936. In that year, the U.S. Army Forces were totally motorized and were the first and only nation to do so until after 1948, although the Army did retain one squadron of horse cavalry in the south west and three pack artillery battalions for mountain use. Tanks were still not considered of much worth as illustrated by the following story as told in <u>War as I Knew It</u> by General George Patton and <u>Patton, Ordeal and Triumph</u> by Ladislas Farago. It seems that Patton, then a Major of Cavalry, had built, at his expense, a tank chassis with motor, tracks, and controls but neither armor nor guns. His purpose was to demonstrate that a tank could be easily maneuvered and maintained. He asked for a group of senior Army Officers to see a demonstration. Patton explained how the tank could be manufactured for durability and ease of use. To show just how simple it was to drive, he asked his wife, Bea, to drive it about the course; she did so easily. Upon completion of Patton's demonstration, the viewing officers all declared it would be of little use in actual combat. Thereupon they mounted their horses and "rode off into the sunset." This all happened some time in the 1920's so Patton returned to his Cavalry Unit and proceeded to forget all about tanks, although tanks did not die, however. Some time between 1924 and 1936, Patton attended the French Cavalry School where he heard DeGaulle lecture on proper use of tanks, which were along the lines of his previous thoughts on tank usage. This lecture piqued his interest once again, but America still had only a few tanks, most of which were hold-overs from World War I, since top commanders were still not convinced of their usefulness.

Later, another action unfolded concerning Patton. He had married the daughter of a wealthy New England industrialist. The newly-weds were deeply committed to each other and both liked horses. The story goes that while George Patton was an accomplished horseman and rider who liked polo, his wife was even a better rider than he. Patton always organized a polo team wherever he was stationed, and the team always elected him its captain. One time while their team was playing for the Army's championship before General Drum, Patton became his usual self — cursing their horses and team members. This explosion was just too much for General Drum who stopped the match and ordered Patton off the field. To the embarrassment of Drum, Patton's team members declared that if Patton could not play neither would they, so in order to finish the match, Drum had to back down. He privately declared, however, that when he became Army Chief-of-Staff, he would summarily dismiss Patton. No officer should use such language. As luck would have it, General George C. Marshall became Chief-of-Staff rather than Drum. Marshall knew well of Patton's ability and daring, so of course retained him.

Then came the German Blitzkrieg of May-June 1940, followed shortly by General Rommel's North African exploits. By this time, many military strategists and Patton began to re-think about Army tanks. Using voice radio in and between tanks and tank commanders, instant communication was feasible. Patton and others realized that if Armored Commanders were forward in their lines where they could observe the action first hand, they could take aggressive action when and where needed. Generals Guderian and Rommel had led the way in using tanks first. From the time Patton first entered the North Africa theater, the German General Staff recognized him as its only chief antagonist, and delegated a field grade officer to observe and keep a current file on Patton's every move, since he not only created fear in their ranks, but also professional admiration.

This brings us to our Tenth Armored Division's action in the War. The Division made use of all the tactical wisdom and instant radio communication then available. Our leaders stressed and lived the axiom of being up front where the action was, so that our commanders quickly could take advantage of every opportunity. Added to this was the fact that General Morris and several senior officers had fought the Germans over the same ground as they had in World War I so they understood the way the Germans would act in any given situation. With all these advantages plus our Task Force Team concept, we were an elite force by all standards!

51
Mansueto

In 1942 and 1943 the long reach of Uncle Sam swept into military service just about every male between the ages of eighteen and thirty-nine years of age. One of these draftees was Mansueto who was of Filipino descent. He was a very bright and independent young man of about thirty-five.

Like some of his peers, he was a Gentlemen's Gentleman or personal valet to a wealthy industrialist, who thought highly of Manse's ability as his servant for he was indeed an excellent one. After Manse had been drafted, the industrialist wrote to the Commanding General of the area where Manse was assigned. He did not want Manse to be hurt or killed in combat for the simple reason that he wanted Manse back to be his personal valet once the war was concluded. This was all done without Manse knowing.

It just so happened that his letter was delivered to General W.H.H. Morris, Jr., who later was to lead the Tenth Armored Division in Europe. General Morris was delighted to receive this letter and so had Manse sent to him for an interview. As both of them struck it off well, General Morris had orders cut transferring Manse to his Headquarters. From that day until General Morris was ordered back from the European Theater to the United States in October, 1945, Manse served him well.

I first got to know Manse when I became General Morris'

aide. Manse took excellent care of the General's clothes, boots, and his quarters. Everything was always cleaned, shined, and well laid out. About the time our Division hit Fort Drient at Metz, the Division's Ordinance Battalion had fitted out one of their small arms repair vans as a mobile office, wardrobe, dressing room, and sleeping quarters for General Morris. He slept there all except one or two nights during the remainder of the War. In the van Manse held complete control in carrying out the General's wishes. Accompanying all his good qualities, Manse did have a fiery disposition if crossed.

Major Walter S. Barnes, Division Headquarters Commandant, and I always got along well with Manse but this was not true of some other Division Headquarters Company officers. One instance comes to mind in particular; it concerns a young second lieutenant whose name I have mercifully forgotten. Our Division's Headquarters had been ordered to move again to another forward location, an action which occurred almost every day. I just happened to be walking by the General's van in time to witness the following scene.

The lieutenant had notified Manse to load up and prepare to move out. Manse, being a very careful and methodical person, prepared to move and so fastened in place for the bumpy ride a chair and other items. At the rear of the van, were several steps and above them was a tarp held up by the roof and two poles. This was a precautionary measure to keep these steps from becoming slippery in wet weather. At this point, the lieutenant returned to find that Manse had not yet loaded the poles and tarp, whereupon he began to toss the poles into the rear of the van. As I stated, Manse had a fiery temper at times. No sooner had these poles hit the van floor than Manse fired them right back outside at the lieutenant. Then he became angry also.

Recognizing this explosive situation, I told the lieutenant to move on and I would take care of the rest of the loading with Manse. He was glad to do so and left. I stuck my head in the van door and asked Manse how I could help, and reminded him that we really must hurry so we could move out with the column. After a few well chosen explicatives, he cooled down and I proceeded to hand him the poles and tarp which he placed carefully on the floor wedging them to prevent the load shifting. He then climbed into the assistant driver's seat and the regular driver moved the van into his assigned spot in the line of march on time.

Over the years this incident has brought smiles to me each time my memory recalled it. Perhaps because I had been privileged to be an enlisted man prior to becoming an officer, I have always felt this fact gave me an insight in treating all men with dignity and respect. Most enlisted men either did not have the education required, nor the opportunity, nor desire, and in some cases the ability to become an officer. Most certainly many were intelligent and decent men who would do most anything for an officer if they knew what and why something had to be done. It is an officer's job to see that these men knew how, when and why concerning their duties.

52
Wounded — But Unbowed?

In an almost inexplicable way, all of our lives became entwined in preparation for and during World War II. This is especially true for those of us who called ourselves "Tigers" of that great Tenth Armored Division as it was truly the vanguard for General Patton and the nemesis of the Nazi. My experiences in that Division were probably a little different from those experienced by soldiers in other good American Army Units.

All of us worked hard to learn the difficult lessons of any war over here in order to acquit ourselves and our units commendably in conflict later. In so doing, we experienced both great drama and terrible travail.

We were told when attacking never to stop to give aid to a fallen soldier. The reason was clear. To do so would make one a stationary target for the enemy, since one could well be killed or wounded by so doing. But how could one not stop to help one's buddy? In spite of all our training, one did anyway. That fellow soldier or officer was closer to you than your own blood brother or sister. One had spent at least a year in training over here. Sweating out those twenty mile hikes, swimming with full packs across cold rivers, sharing our food and drink in the heat of summer or cold of winter, and now we were "over there"!

As I knelt one time beside my badly injured friend, I realized that his time for this world was extremely short. Since he was only able to lift a hand feebly, I took his in mine and with his last breath he asked me to tell his family "that he loved them!" I solemnly swore to him I would do so knowing all the while before the sun set that very day, I also might be lying in the snow and mud making that same request of another fellow Tiger. As I repeated the Lord's Prayer and the Twenty Third Psalm, his eye lids fluttered as he "Quietly folded his tent and stole away".

I have never thought of myself as sentimental. My dear wife, Shirley, will tell you that for the first several years of our marriage in the middle of a sound sleep, I would suddenly sit bolt-upright in a cold sweat. She would gently lay her hand on my back asking "another bad memory?" I'd say "yes", and bolt out of bed to walk the floor for twenty to thirty minutes to settle down once again. Only then was it possible to return to bed and restful sleep. For years, I could not face going to our Tenth Armored Division's reunions. The memories of lost comrades were too painful; now we both go and would not think of missing them. It has been many years since the re-occurrence of those sleep interruptions. Still, during those quiet moments in the dark of night, memories come flooding back.

When we were still in final training stages at Camp Gordon, Georgia, our "B" Battery of Four Hundred Twenty Third Armored Field Artillery Battalion had another Second Lieutenant in it. His home was in rural Georgia. Two of his favorite expressions were: "When this War is over I'm going to return home and raise chickens and children.", and the other, "When we get over there and we hear a sound like the breaking of concrete, — duck.". This Lieutenant loved to talk and even though he ranked me as a Second Lieutenant, I openly accused him of falling in the battery just so he could have someone to talk to. At times, I felt sorry for those enlisted men as they had to stand and listen to all his diatribe, since having been an enlisted man myself for a short time, I could empathize with them. After the Division returned home, he went back to the farm he so dearly loved. Apparently, he had "ducked" as there were no apparent injuries he sustained. Like some of the rest of us, he was lucky. Some years ago, Captain Owen McBride, our Battery Commander, informed me that this same Lieutenant committed suicide about six months after becoming a civilian farmer again.

After being released from active duty late in 1945, I returned home, and during that happy Christmas Season, I kept feeling my left ear. I felt a little hard lump on the top rim of my ear, so finally I mentioned it to my Dad. At first he could see nothing and so jokingly passed it off by saying that I was probably growing "horns". After a couple of more days, I could discern a sharp point there. It was then that he got out his magnifying glass to have a better look. With his needle-nose pliers, he extracted a small piece of shrapnel about one fourth inch long and the size of a needle. I knew that I had been close to repeated explosions of shells and bombs besides all the other small arms fire but never once did I feel anything like being hit with shrapnel. I was as surprised as he was at this outcome. If one is cognizant of how pieces of shrapnel act in the human body, one realizes that, because those fragments are razor sharp as well as jagged, they work through one's flesh. I was lucky as this one, even though small, worked its way out at the top of my ear. Had it gone inward, it very well in time could have caused blindness or deafness or cut the motor centers of my brain leaving me partially paralyzed.

To be eligible for the Purple Heart, one must be stricken on the battlefield and then go, or be taken to an aid station for treatment. I qualified as to the former, but not for the latter. Naturally I was glad to have been spared serious injury so I never received the honor of joining that distinguished fraternity of the Purple Hearts.

We had not been in the Seventh Army very long when one of the most tragic of tactical misjudgments occurred. In 1945 Higher Headquarters had correctly assigned a primary target deep in the enemy held territory, as the bull's eye we were to hit. In every armored attack such a primary target was assigned to our Armored Division, and rightly so. This, like all such primary targets was referred to as a "goose egg" and was always over or around a main railroad and/or a road junction or an essential bridge. This goose egg, as always, was several miles ahead of our present front lines. Higher Headquarters also assigned several secondary areas to be taken between our present lines and our main target. All these tactics were done properly.

Our Division had just recently shifted to the Seventh Army from Patton's Third Army and we continued the same fierce tactics that carried us forward so successfully in Patton's Army. We vigorously launched our attack at dawn, broke through the enemy lines in short order, rolled up his local reserves and artillery, and by 1200 hours were fast approaching the primary target area or goose egg. It was then General Morris radioed a message to Higher Headquarters asking for the next primary target for our Division. In the meantime all of those secondary targets were being taken. The radio operator at Corp Headquarters acknowledged our signal and said, "Roger. Wait.". So we waited. As we were fast closing in on our primary target, General Morris again repeated his signal with the added note that if further instructions were not received quickly he would have to coil our Division in, on, and around the primary target. Again Corp replied, "Roger. Wait.".

With no further instructions, General Morris could do nothing except "coil" our Division, as he stated. We were forced to sit there three hours before Seventh Army or Corp could decide what to do with us! General Morris was indeed disgruntled with this long delay.

When we <u>did</u> receive our orders, they were totally unbelievable! We were ordered to return to the place in line where we had begun our attack early that morning. Also, our Division was to return over the very same road we had just attacked. This was sheer madness.

Looking back on this event, I can understand now that the Seventh Army was to echelon to their right and be the connecting link between Patton's fast moving Army on the Seventh's left flank and the slower moving First French Army on the right flank. In spite of all this, there was no reason to send us back on that identical road, for the results of this order were for us to take a beating as the Germans had time to move up artillery, heavy mortars, and 88's. That afternoon, the only enemy air attacks against the Allied lines were directed at us, so we caught it all. Our Division was forced to thread our way back through this blazing path. By going forward in our earlier attack, we lost few men and vehicles, but coming back we lost many men and much equipment.

What our orders should have read would be to return by swinging to either right or left flank. This would have allowed us freedom of movement to attack and kill a lot of the enemy's reserves and reserve artillery as we returned; then they would have been the target instead of us. Naturally, the enemy air activity would have been little different except that our units would have been scattered instead of concentrated, thereby offering more difficult targets to attack.

To me, this was one of the two worst orders given us during the War. It spoke loudly of ignorance by Higher Headquarters of the proper use of armor. This error never could have happened in Patton's Army. All his higher Unit Commanders, as well as their staffs, knew how to use armor effectively.

During this return-to-line operation, enemy air was strafing our columns with machine guns, 20 mm. cannon fire, and one hundred pound bombs. Captain Harry Carl, Battery Commander of "C" Battery Four Hundred Twenty Third Armored Field Artillery Battalion was riding in his half-track. The assistant driver was operating their fifty caliber machine guns against these air attacks. Captain Carl, seeing how close enemy fire came to his track, ordered him to take cover and he took over. He fired on the next attacking plane at the same moment the enemy pilot dropped his bomb.

Captain E.O. McBride, "B" Battery Commander, explained that his "B" half-track was just ahead of the "C" Battery half-track. Actually an anti-personnel bomb was dropped and landed between these two vehicles. Captain

McBride's half-track, like all of our half-tracks, had a steel rack welded on the rear and outside of it. (Incidentally, those steel racks welded onto the outside of our half-tracks were used originally to carry our Air Corp bombs overseas by ships. After the bombs had been removed these steel racks were thrown away. We found them in an Air Corp dump and used them to good advantage.) Into this was placed all their bed rolls and other duffel. This arrangement kept the inside of this vehicle clear for men to move around and fight. The bomb's shrapnel was stopped by all those bed rolls and so no one was injured in the "B" half-track.

The "C" half-track was not so fortunate as the bomb blast sent shrapnel smashing against the fifty caliber machine gun mount ricocheting into Captain Carl's head and neck. The result of this attack was a long recuperation for Captain Carl. Even today, nearly fifty years latter, Harry Carl has intense headaches. Although medication helps, he has suffered much all these years.

When one asks the question: "Were we wounded — yet unbowed?" What say you?

53
Our Fifty Fifth Engineers

Among the several unusual and fine projects that our Division Engineers completed in combat, three stand above all the rest, in my opinion. One was their leadership in envisaging and constructing a road through mountains which by-passed the German's at Zerf Corner and the "Bowling Alley". The other was planking railroad bridges so that tanks in our Division with "duck bills" could safely cross over rivers and ravines. This later activity was necessary to allow those tanks having "duck bills" to cross without hang-ups on the railroad rails. What are "duck bills"? They are extensions on the tracks. The third project was mine clearing.

You may recall that our Division had crossed the swollen Saar River, in early 1944, by using a pontoon bridge which the Ninety Fourth Infantry Division had built. We then enlarged our bridge-head through the Siegfried Line of pill-boxes, stormed eastward through the German defenses to the Zerf road junction, then turned abruptly north to try to capture all three bridges intact at Trier. As we turned northward at Zerf, this road lay in a deep valley and the enemy was on the heights all along its eastern side. They were looking down directly on us and could shoot with direct 88 fire the entire length of this road. Colonel Richardson's Task Force had rushed north on this road but as he did so, the Nazis began building up their direct fire capabilities, hence we called this road the "Bowling Alley".

After sizing up the danger to our men traveling through this "Bowing Alley", plus the difficulty of moving needed supplies to support them, our Engineers began to study the mountain valley which lay to the west as an alternate route north toward Trier. They used bulldozers and tank dozers to cut this northward road out of rock and forest. Once this road was leveled, we used it exclusively as it was in defilade from German guns, thus saving many lives. Who but our Engineers could have conceived and constructed such a road!

"Duck bills" were small steel extensions about five inches long fastened to some of our tank tracks to increase flotation in spongy and swampy terrain. Our Engineers not only had to measure the width of bridges we might have to cross but also to determine whether they could support those thirty-five ton brutes. Bridges for our tanks with "duck bills" had to be wider than those necessary for our tanks without them. Division G-3 had to know bridge widths to maneuver their tanks accordingly. If bridges were not strong enough to carry tank traffic, then they had to be strengthened as well. Should an existing railroad bridge be considered for use, it had to be planked before tanks equipped with "duck bills" could cross, otherwise the tanks would hang up on the rails and thus impede our crossing.

There was a third alternate for which I also admired our Engineers. This consisted of locating tank (Teller) mine fields and removing or exploding them usually under small arms and mortar fire. This method resulted in perilous situations made still more hazardous because this operation took place in front of the Switch Position of the Siegfried Line between the Saar and Mosel Rivers. I was glad then when the Twentieth Corp pulled us out of that line and sent us north to hit the southern flank of Von Rundstedt's Army. Then I discovered that we had jumped from the frying pan into the fire.

So nevertheless, three cheers to our Division's great Engineers!

54
White Crosses

In 1989 my wife and I returned once again to the rolling hills and ridges of Bastogne. Memories flooded over me of those earlier desperate days in mid-December, 1944 when our Tenth Armored Division met and stalled Von Rundstedt's drive north and westward toward the port of Antwerp, Belgium. Today those green rolling hills are peaceful, filled only with grazing farm animals and verdant crops. The thrifty little town of Bastogne now sleeps quietly in the summer sunshine. In December, 1944 it presented a different scene with windows and roofs shattered, walls pockmarked with bullet and shrapnel wounds, and around every corner a tank gun or machine gun. Then the snow drifted softly down as if to try and hide man's ugly destruction.

Later that summer's day in 1989, we visited the American National Military Cemetery at Hamm, Luxembourg, which is located about five miles south and east of Luxembourg City. Like all such American National Cemeteries overseas, it is kept immaculately. This one had five thousand white crosses, row on row, set upon an absolutely flat perfectly manicured green lawn. The only distinguishing difference of one white cross (or Star of David) from the next was the name of that soldier who rested below. No rank was printed, just a name. Even General Patton was treated this way.

At the entrance and slightly above on a three foot burm

was a small chapel whose dark marble walls were in contrast to the green turf. This chapel was only about twenty-five feet square. The threshold of its door and the floor beyond were filled with great armloads of flowers. Besides this chapel and separate from it was a marble wall about ten feet high by twenty feet long. On one side were several maps etched into it illustrating the Battle of the Bulge with its various stages and dates. On the other side of this wall were engraved the names of two hundred and fifty men who were missing in action from those great battles. The entire cemetery was serenely quiet and awe-inspiring, very beautiful in its simplicity. I must admit tears welled up in my eyes as I viewed those crosses and read their names. In the trees all around this cemetery, birds were singing sweetly.

The surprising fact that day was not those armloads of flowers at the chapel. These had been given by various American and Military Associations in fond memory to those men buried here. As one viewed those crosses, every now and then there was single red carnation laid at its base. After all those years, the ordinary people of Bastogne and Luxembourg still remembered a man from a far country who had given his "all" for their freedom. They are the persons who annually presented him a red carnation in eternal tribute. True, in many cases it was their children or grandchildren who honored this fallen American with a red carnation. These stories and exploits had been handed down from one generation to the next of how this G.I. had befriended them and driven off their German tyrant only to lose his life in so doing. In their hearts he had insured their liberty once again. He asked nothing in return.

The persons in charge of our American cemeteries in Europe tell us that even now, nearly fifty years later, one or two G.I.'s bodies are found in the Ardens Forest from that great battle. These remains are usually stumbled upon by a forester or hiker. Often a hard rain will wash away the forest duff exposing a skeleton with bits of uniform. The nearest American authority is then notified. A burial team arrives and carefully removes this man's bones being careful to save all possible identification. He then will be taken to Frankfort, Germany to be identified, usually by dental plates. Once this move has been accomplished, he will be placed into a coffin and transported to one of our American Military Cemeteries, usually in Belgium, for burial. In the meantime his nearest of kin now living will be advised of his recovery and exactly when and where the internment will take place with full military honors. This gives his family a chance to be present for this service.

I know of no other nation who gave so much magnanimously for some one else's freedom as did the United States. Then when the fighting ceased we helped even our former enemies rebuild their homeland. The only other country that would come close to this would, of course, be Great Britain but England had terrible devastation at home so their help was limited. May each of us in our heart of hearts be as eternally grateful for those lads now at rest in Hamm and other American National Cemeteries.

So once again we see white crosses row on row above beautiful green turf. Only the names are different.

55
The Rose Garden

Rose gardens always attract birds and bees — and often people. This particular rose garden was no exception. In this case, however, the persons attracted happen to be American G.I.'s, more specifically one platoon of "A" Company of our Fifty Fifth Armored Engineer Battalion, Tenth Armored Division.

This story was related to me recently by Richard Malone of that platoon. It seems they ended combat in World War II in Garmish-Partenkirchen, Germany, even more specifically, this unit was billeted in a house #4 on Hoelzeweg Street in Partenkirchen. Richard Malone had returned home to the U.S.A. after the War where he spent six years earning his advanced degree in finance and foreign service studies. Some time later he was hired by the American Express firm and returned once more to Germany where he managed their business and financial ventures in all of Germany.

During this time, he met and married a German girl from Garmish-Partenkirchen. In sitting around visiting with her family, the subject of rose gardens came up. Malone explained that he and his platoon buddies had been billeted at the close of hostilities in a home in Partenkirchen that had an especially beautiful rose garden. In chorus his wife's aunt and uncle explained the "family Hohenlactner's" rose garden was indeed the most beautiful and famous rose garden in all that city. Her aunt and uncle knew it well having often visited with Mr. and

Mrs. Hohenleitner in their lovely home and had enjoyed their roses many times.

Hearing this story Malone became a bit alarmed and told his bride and her aunt and uncle that no one should "dig very deeply" in that lovely rose garden. They wanted to know why. His explanation was simple.

It seems that his platoon had carried the usual full complement of demolitions in their half-tracks. On 8 May, 1945 at the end of combat, they had been directed to haul these explosives some distance and turn them over to our ordinance for proper disposal. Being young and oh-so-glad the fighting was over, they decided to dig a large hole in that rose garden and bury all these demolitions there, being careful to replant the roses as nearly as possible to their original site, thus giving the appearance of the roses not having been disturbed. This action saved several hours of time for them and enabled them to relax and enjoy themselves as opposed to driving many miles, waiting in line with other troops to turn over their explosives.

Upon hearing this news, his wife's family were terrified for their friends and their roses. They promptly notified the local police who in turn phoned the German Bomb Disposal Unit in Munich. Very shortly thereafter, this bomb disposal squad arrived with all necessary equipment and special trucks. Using steel rods and metal detectors, they located the catch and began to dig cautiously. They potted each rose plant and set it aside. First, of course, they had the local police clear a city block surrounding that rose garden just to be safe.

They then removed several hundred pounds of TNT, cases of tank mines, boxes of anti-personnel mines, cases of hand grenades, white phosphorous grenades, thermal grenades, many bangalor torpedoes, cases of bazooka rockets, several boxes of .30 and .50 caliber machine gun ammunition, and legions of trip wires, and pressure fuses, plus primer cord. Altogether that day, the German bomb squad excavated four truck loads of this dangerous material without accident. Probably the most dangerous of all were the bazooka rockets.

After this, the Holenleitner family replaced their lovely roses and settled down once again to a peaceful life. As everyone loves roses, I just felt you would enjoy learning about this particular "rose garden".

56
Twenty One Dollars Per Month

Like all young Privates in the Army, I was paid eighteen dollars per month. Shortly after I enlisted, our Congress, in a burst of generosity, voted us a pay raise of three green backs to twenty-one dollars per month.

With all this new found affluence, what did we spend it on? After all our food, housing and clothing were furnished by Uncle Sam. As best I can recall when we presented ourselves to the Paymaster, he deducted eight dollars and ninety cents for our ten thousand dollar G.I. life insurance policy. The balance was handed to us in cash after we signed his receipt record. This tremendous sum of sixteen dollars and ten cents was all ours for good or ill and had to last out that month. How did we spend this?

In those days we went once or twice a week to the post flick at fifteen cents per movie. A postcard was one cent and first class postage only three cents. Gasoline was fifteen cents per gallon, if you were lucky enough to find some. After purchasing some toothpaste and shaving soap, the rest of our money we sent home where our family carefully hoarded it in a bank savings account which paid the magnificent sum of one percent interest. Every other month my parents would purchase a twenty-five dollar War Bond for eighteen dollars and seventy-five cents from that bank account. This bond paid about three percent if kept ten years. At least is was better than the one

percent which the banks paid. Each of our 105 mm. rounds cost
Uncle Sam twenty-five dollars. We paid only eighteen dollars
and seventy-five cents for each twenty-five dollar War Bond and
one bond did not even purchase one round of artillery. War is
costly in every way.

In those day, our Congress voted themselves a <u>reduction</u>
in their pay due to the War. Today everyone in Washington
appears to grab all they can get. It's a far cry from 1942 - 1945
when even the politicians helped the common cause of winning
the War. Today, first class mail is twenty-nine cents and
gasoline has just gone up to one dollar sixteen cents per gallon.
In spite of little money, we all had enough to eat and clothes to
wear. There are moments when I almost wished for the return
of those days financially.

The question has often been asked just what was life like
over there in combat. The three "F's" come to mind. They were
fatigue, frustration and fear! Fatigue because of lack of sleep;
often we slept on the ground in snow or mud and other times a
hard stone floor or cellar became our bedstead. It was almost
impossible to find a comfortable place to sleep. What sleep we
did get was fitful at best. Added to this was the enemy
interdicting fire into our area all night long. It was their habit
to fire artillery or mortar or machine guns every half hour. By
doing this they hoped to accomplish two objectives. The first,
was to disrupt our rest and second, they might just be lucky and
hit a gasoline truck or dump or ammunition truck. Now and
then they did.

Getting only three or four hours of sleep in twenty-four
eventually drained one's stamina. In my case, it also caused

severe headaches. To counteract this pain, the medics gave me a bottle of A.P.C. (caffeine and aspirin) to help relieve my problem. After several weeks even this did not help.

Now we come to our second problem called frustration. Imagine everything you try to do is beset and stymied by mud, snow, fog, wind, rain, freezing cold or intense heat. Then add the lack of sleep plus very few hot meals. Meals generally were catch-as-catch-can, seldom more than twice a day with "K" rations inbetween. The "K" ration was the Army's high energy candy bar. A man could eat only a bite or two at a time as they were very rich with chocolate and heavily loaded with wax so they would not melt easily. Along with all of this, the physical daily effort to load and unload and carry cases of rifle and machine gun ammunition plus five gallon cans of gasoline, five gallons of water, drums of oil and lubricants and thousands of rounds of artillery and mortar shells was exhausting. Every action plus incoming fire added to our frustration.

Every officer and man in the United States Third Army (Patton's) was required to shave daily. The officers also had to wear a tie. Personally, I shaved every day by simply unbuttoning my shirt collar and loosening my tie. My shaving was always using my tin hat with cold water and regular soap which irritated my face. The other daily ritual consisted of removing my boots and socks, rubbing my feet with G.I. foot powder, then putting on a dry (if possible) pair of socks. The ones I just removed, I placed inside my shirt to dry for the next day. This process was known as the "Admiral Byrd technique". It seems that when he was in the Arctic alone for several weeks, and someone later asked him how he kept clean, his answer was that he wore the first shirt until the could not stand it any longer then he removed it and stood it in the corner of his hut to "air out"; when the second shirt became intolerable he switched. This is what all of us did with our socks.

Even though I became a Division Commanding General's Aide, I did not have the opportunity to remove my clothes and take a bath for six weeks. On returning home after the War, I tried to get rid of the body odor in my two good wool shirts. They were dry cleaned several times, washed in Woolite and hung out to air for weeks, all to no avail. I had to destroy them. Sanitation is almost impossible at the front lines. Also there is little or no privacy.

The last item is fear which is self evident. In World War I, seventy percent of all losses of men were caused by artillery. I do not know what the ratio was for World War II, but it was probably close to that figure. Fear adds to fatigue and frustration.

Fear generally came under three headings: fear of being lost, fear of death, and fear of being wounded. Only one time do I recall being disoriented or lost for a short time overseas. Generally speaking, this fear was of minor importance in Continental Europe.

Fear of death was very real, however. One need ask oneself what is it about death that causes such a fear? Several thoughts or emotions surface. We fear losing the gentle kindness and love of family members. The thought of permanent and sudden separation evokes pain. Next is the uncertainty of the unknown future. Here we get into deeper water. In combat, each of us agonized over our personal death possibility.

The last of our fears was also very real. The fear of being badly wounded never leaves one. From the very first action, this fear was exacerbated as all around us men had legs and arms blown off by personal mines and/or shells; grievous cuts and puncture wounds; and sudden loss of sight or hearing. Those killed instantly were the "lucky" ones. Graphic details need not be recited to convey this all pervasive fear. It shadowed one constantly, day and night. These fears also added greatly to one's fatigue.

The last of our concerns was boredom. War consists of periods of intense activity often interrupted by periods of inaction. After the second or third time one has cleaned and checked one's weapon and its ammunition, one becomes bored.

Some of us carried Testaments or prayer books which we read. Other men had left theirs in their duffle bags at the rear. I have seen men read the backs of cigarette packs or K-rations several times over just to have something to do. Still others closed their eyes to better envision their family back home, including their mother removing a hot apple pie from the oven. They could almost smell and taste it. Still others fretted over their personal danger from impending attacks. All the previously mentioned fears including boredom reinforces one's fatigue.

"D.D.T." powder had become the be-all-to-end-all for fleas and bugs overseas. Most of us carried a shaker can of it in our duffel. I was no exception. To prevent bites and infestations from these critters, most of us dusted our long underwear with "D.D.T.". Additionally, whenever we were forced to sleep in a probable location, we also dusted our bed roll. To maintain personal sanitation most men kept their hair very short. In my case it was bout 3/8 inch long. Only once all the time we were in Europe did I awaken to feel something crawling in my hair. It was a bed bug which I quickly squashed and then I dusted my hair and bedding with "D.D.T.".

Having been through all of this in combat with the fine troops of our great Tenth Armored Division, I fail to comprehend why some nice American young women would ever wish to be in the combat forces of our Army.

57
Intelligence

Intelligence of the enemy is decisive to the success of a well run Division. General Morris, our Tenth Armored Tiger Division Commanding General, insisted that we give him just the "facts" about the enemy. "Do not try to tell me what I want to hear or butter me up with your assumptions."

Now the word "assume" is an excellent English word. It is the root word of assumption. My dictionary defines it: "to arrogate to oneself; to usurp; to pretend or affect; to take for granted". Our General had a classic way to interpret this word. If you write it as follows: "Ass-u-me", it says to assume something as a fact, it makes an ass of you and me. "Never assume anything about the enemy; just give me the brutal facts either ill or good." "You must disregard the "good old boy" network, i.e. what class ring they wear, and rumors. Should there be rumors, dig until you discover the facts."

In our Division Headquarters, we had the regular G-2 Section which is totally concerned with enemy intelligence. Lieutenant Colonel "Bill" Eckles was our G-2. Here was a man of great mental acumen, a man whose word was his bond. He was friendly and personable but beneath his surface appearance he was a shaker and mover. When our Division first received its rush orders to move into East and Northern Luxembourg to attack the Germans at the Bulge, General Morris instantly sent Bill Eckles north to find out what the Germans were up to. In his jeep with his driver, they drove north into that country. Because of the dark of night, snow squalls, and confused situation, Bill's jeep overshot friendly lines. The Germans literally shot the jeep from under him. Shaken but unhurt, he scrambled out of the wreckage, commandeered another jeep, carried out his mission, and returned to tell General Morris the "facts".

To assist our G-2 Section, Third Army assigned some special additional personnel, Second Lieutenant Moss was one of these persons. Moss actually was a German Jew who barely escaped the clutches of the dreaded Gustopo. He had fled with the aid of the French underground but they could not save his sister who was taken to one of the death camps. Moss was about twenty-three years of age at that time. After he left the European Continent, he worked his way to the U.S.A. and immediately volunteered his services to the Army. Obviously we were delighted to have a man who had lived all his life in Germany and could speak the language fluently. After he completed Officers School, Third Army assigned him to our Division as an "interrogator". In spite of all the agony Germany had inflicted upon his family, he never held a grudge against their soldiers.

His method of operation was low key. An enemy soldier or officer would be ushered into his little office and after the usual salutes were exchanged, he offered a chair and an American cigarette. In this relaxed atmosphere, Moss asked oblique questions, getting men to talk about their lives. He seldom took their statements at face value. However, on one occasion that I can recall and after getting what he felt were incorrect answers, he had those P.O.W.s moved to a different barn. Fresh straw had been placed inside for the P.O.W.s to rest upon. Before this straw had been placed, he had microphones hidden. He would listen through earphones next door. On this particular instance the German P.O.W.s told him one story during the interview but upon being returned to confinement they bragged among themselves about how they had misled Moss. Moss heard the true "facts" at last. His subterfuge was beautiful!

Still another unit that was assigned to our G-2 Section by Third Army was the Order-of-Battle team. Captain Walter Dee headed this team and he had two Tech Sergeants to assist him. Their job was to sift through all data concerning the enemy which included Moss's reports, captured documents, our patrol, and reconnaissance units reports. Walter Dee spoke and read the Polish, Russian, German and French languages. His sergeants spoke German, French, Italian and Dutch. Walter's team reduced all this great mass of data to simple, easily understood facts, i.e. what German units were in front of us, where their main mass of troops were, where their reserves were, how large these forces were, their armaments, morale, and state of training.

Over all of this effort, Bill Eckles held a tight reign. When all this data was combined with the intelligence reports of Third Army plus adjacent units including air photos, an excellent picture appeared. All of the above was upgraded continuously and recorded on the situation map in our Forward Division's War Room.

General Morris needed "the facts" to be able to direct our

strength toward the enemy's weak spots. Once again our Tenth Armored Tiger Division would claw large chunks out of those enemy troops before us.

"Just give me the facts", he repeated.

Lt. Col. LaFlour   Lt. Col. Wm. Eckles   Capt. Plowman   Lt. Col. Laudig   Lt. Chapman
Judge Advocate   Intelligence   Military Government   Personnel   Aide

ROAD TO THE FUTURE

Bright dreams, high hopes and prayer
    These are our tools in hand
By which to build a road more fair
    In God's war weary land.

Not as a conquering, vengeful horde
    Must we our pathways lay
By using truth and justice as our sword
    Hew to His way.

One little hour to build
    And after that we close
Our book of life with dreams still unfulfilled
    To find repose.

Yet in the future men may see our dreams
    And build aright
And things which now so futile seem
    Yield to their might.

Laurel O. Poole

TIMELESS QUESTIONS FOR A LEADER

From the book entitled <u>Foch Speaks</u> by Major Charles Bugnet
    Published by MacVeagh, 19298
    (Permission by Longman Group U.K.)

What is the <u>real</u> question?
Whatever you do, you must do it well,
    no matter how unimportant it is.

To know a trade one must learn it.
One must take exercise and lead a regular life.
The power to get things done calls for certain
    qualities: intelligence, judgment,
    imagination, and decision.

When one knows what one wills, everything
    becomes easy.
One must act, it is only that, which produces
    results.
One's value consists of what one does.

DIVISION HEADQUARTERS WITH DATES

Arrived	Destination	Departed
	Left pier at New York on "Alexander" and was grounded same night in harbor.	11 Sep. 44
	Transferred by ferry-boat to the "Brazil" and left that afternoon about five o'clock.	12 Sep. 44
	Caught up with our convoy.	20 Sep. 44
22 Sep. 44	Anchored in Weymouth, England Harbor	
23 Sep. 44	Cherbourg and Teurtheville, France	24 Oct. 44
27 Oct. 44	Passed thru Paris, France	
29 Oct. 44	Mars La Tours, France	9 Nov. 44
9 Nov. 44	Ottange, France	16 Nov. 44
16 Nov. 44	Petite Hettange, France	19 Nov. 44
19 Nov. 44	Laumesfeld, France	21 Nov. 44
21 Nov. 44	Apach, France	17 Dec. 44
17 Dec. 44	Luxembourg City	23 Dec. 44
23 Dec. 44	Mersch, Luxembourg	26 Dec. 44
26 Dec. 44	Metz, France	17 Jan. 45
17 Jan. 45	Dieuze, France	22 Jan. 45
22 Jan. 45	Falquemont, France	10 Feb. 45
10 Feb. 45	Metz, France	19 Feb. 45
19 Feb. 45	Apach, France	22 Feb. 45
22 Feb. 45	Wincheringen, Germany	23 Feb. 45
23 Feb. 45	Ayl, Germany	27 Feb. 45
27 Feb. 45	Irsch, Germany	1 Mar. 45
1 Mar. 45	Steinbach, Germany	2 Mar. 45
2 Mar. 45	Trier, Germany	9 Mar. 45
9 Mar. 45	Ehrang, Germany	11 Mar. 45
11 Mar. 45	Trier, Germany	17 Mar. 45
17 Mar. 45	Mitlosheim, Germany	18 Mar. 45
18 Mar. 45	Wadern, Germany	19 Mar. 45
19 Mar. 45	St. Wendell, Germany	20 Mar. 45
20 Mar. 45	Kaiserslautern, Germany	23 Mar. 45
23 Mar. 45	Neustadt, Germany	24 Mar. 45
24 Mar. 45	King of Bavaria's summer palace	28 Mar. 45

DIVISION HEADQUARTERS WITH DATES

Arrived	Destination	Departed
28 Mar. 45	Mannheim, Germany	31 Mar. 45
31 Mar. 45	Heidelberg, Germany	2 Apr. 45
2 Apr. 45	Hoffenheim, Germany	4 Apr. 45
4 Apr. 45	Rappanau, Germany	5 Apr. 45
5 Apr. 45	Merchingen, Germany	7 Apr. 45
7 Apr. 45	Assamstadt, Germany	12 Apr. 45
12 Apr. 45	Inglefingen, Germany	13 Apr. 45
13 Apr. 45	Ohringen, Germany	16 Apr. 45
16 Apr. 45	Bubenorbis, Germany	19 Apr. 45
19 Apr. 45	Fichtenberg, Germany	20 Apr. 45
20 Apr. 45	Lorch, Germany	21 Apr. 45
21 Apr. 45	Goppingen, Germany	22 Apr. 45
22 Apr. 45	Westerheim, Germany	23 Apr. 45
23 Apr. 45	Ehingen, Germany	24 Apr. 45
24 Apr. 45	Laupheim, Germany	25 Apr. 45
25 Apr. 45	Dittenheim, Germany	26 Apr. 45
26 Apr. 45	Babenhausen, Germany	27 Apr. 45
27 Apr. 45	Kaufbeuren, Germany	28 Apr. 45
28 Apr. 45	Schongau, Germany	29 Apr. 45
29 Apr. 45	Steingaden, Germany	30 Apr. 45
30 Apr. 45	Garmisch-Partenkirchen, Germany	24 May 45
24 May 45	Igls, Austria	4 Jun. 45

NOTE: A copy of our Tenth Armored Division official
list of locations as of June, 1945 which was
distributed to all concerned.

Copy of H.V. Kaltenborn's Radio Address
November, 1944

Headquarters 10th Armored Division
APO 260   U.S. Army   30 November 1944

The following extract of a radio broadcast to the U.S. by short wave from
Verdein, France, at 0045, 29 Nov. 1944 (2:45 p.m. 28 Nov. New York Time) by
Mr. H.V. Kaltenborn, famed radio announcer, is published for the information of
all personnel:

"Today, I went back into Germany. A little more than five years ago,
two days before this war began, Adolph Hitler sent me out of Germany because
I had told the truth about him. Today I went back in with the Tenth Armored
Division of General Patton's Third Army and Hitler didn't stop me. I got the feel
of his artillery fire, but I also got a good idea of the fighting qualities of the men
who are defeating Hitler's armies.

By spending yesterday as the guest of the Ninth Air Force, and today
as the guest of the 10th Armored Division in the front lines, I got an excellent
idea of that teamwork between our aviation and our ground forces which is
such an important factor in helping us win an unbroken succession of victories
at the lowest possible cost in men. There is little good flying weather on this
front. One day a week is about the average. But the Ninth Air Force has
learned how to make that one day count. This afternoon, the boys of the Tenth
Armored Division who are holding the front lines in Germany, told me how
happy they feel when they see the P47's overhead, preparing the way for the
next advance. "They come close to hitting us sometimes", they said, "but we
sure like to see them".

The Tenth Armored Division of the Third Army was committed to action
in France just two months after leaving an Atlantic port. That was only a few
weeks ago. Yet today it is a veteran battle division which has won nearly a
thousand Purple Hearts in action. It has won every important objective
assigned to it and it has fought against some of the best German divisions on
this front. It was the first division of the Third Army to enter Germany. The
capture a few days ago, of the village of Berthingen was described for me by
the men who planned the action. It was a small action intended to give
Company B of the * * * * * Armored Infantry its first taste of offensive action
under conditions that would make success almost certain. It was a small but
highly coordinated operation. There was minute planning for the use of artillery
and mortars and smoke to blind the enemy. We had superior observation, our
men had carefully trained, they had excellent leaders. What was the result of
the action? The capture of one town, the elimination of a dangerous enemy
observation post, the taking of 38 prisoners, the infliction of unknown enemy
losses in killed and wounded, and the whole operation accomplished at the cost
of one man killed and two men wounded. And Company B has earned its
spurs."

Copy of Earl Mazo of Stars and Stripes Staff - 1944

Tenth Armored "Tigers" Prowl Reich, Despite Trips, Mines.
By Earl Mazo - Stars and Stripes Staff Writer

With Tenth Arm'd Division in Germany - Nov-22-1944. This Division has smashed thru to Germany at several points, and a column this morning was tackling one of the outer defenses of the Siegfried Line west of the Saar between that river and Luxembourg. The Tenth Armored "Tigers" were the first Division of Patton's Third Army to reach Germany.

While there has been opposition aplenty from German troops and artillery, tankers and armored doughboys of this outfit figure their biggest obstacles so far have been of an engineering nature; mines of every description, including concrete "plastic" bounding, and boxwood enclosed Reigel mines, tank ditches and traps at every turn and advantageous spot. Blown bridges and craters are everywhere in the path of the advancing Tenth. At one point a tank slipped on the road shoulder apparently on a double-up mine. It was blown up and fell over on a passing jeep and occupants of the jeep.

In one small field by a road block, engineers uncovered more than 150 mines. During the first part of the advance one armored engineers Lieutenant commanding a platoon in the 55th Engineer Battalion, enraged by the danger to his men of German mines, ordered the GI's into ditches and went alone ahead of the tanks with a mine detector. Later he rode the lead tank of the column and at every suspicious spot stopped and jumped off to work mine detector ahead of the tank.

With columns of the division branching off at one point, the signal men had a hellish time. They worked a straight thirty-six hours laying over three hundred miles of telephone lines alone.

My note - Lts. Dean Chapman of 1224 West. Mich. Ave., Wally Bunt, whose wife the former Yvonne Wilkinson living at 621 N. Sycamore and Billy E. Haull of 1141 N. Logan are with this 10th Arm'd Division.

Little Groups of Yanks Broke Up Big Nazi Push
By Hugh Schuck
(Staff Correspondent of The News)

With the U.S. Third Army, Jan 4 - As details of fighting in the early stages of Field Marshal Karl Von Rundstedt's breakthrough emerge from a shroud of secrecy imposed by disrupted communications and censorship, it becomes more and more aparent that the initial impetus of the German drive was broken by isolated American units which chose to fight to the last cartridge against overwhelming odds.

It was such a last ditch fight by Major General Raymond O. Barton's 4th Infantry Division and part of Major General William H.H. Morris' 10th Armored Division which kept the Germans from capturing the City of Luxembourg and its road network over which Lieutenant General George S. Patton later moved his divisions to launch a counterattack. And it was that kind of American resistance that centered around Berdorf, 17 miles northeast of the city of Luxembourg.

ARMOR SPLIT UP

The 10th Armored Division was the first Third Army unit rushed north to help stem the German tide. By forced march the 10th Armored Division reached Luxembourg on December 17, the day after the attack opened. There it was split, one part being scattered to the northeast to bolster various units, while the rest rushed toward Bastonge.

Incidentally, it was the 10th Armored Division which met the German drive head on outside Bastonge, threw it back on its heels and saved the city. The 10th Armored repulsed attack after attack in eight hours of continuous battle before the first elements of the 101st Airborne entered the city and joined in its defense. Ironically, the 101st got credit for the defense of Bastonge because censorship permitted it to be mentioned before the 10th Armored Division.

Berdorf was nearly encircled the morning of December 18 when two platoons of tanks and two of armored infantry from the 10th drove through heavy artillery fire to reinforce two companies of the 12th Infantry Regiment of the 4th Division, which had been holding out there.

Then for three days this force of about 150 men commanded by Captain Steve Lang of Chicago, threw back the best the Germans had to offer, killing 350 of the enemy and destroying large numbers of German tanks and armored vehicles, while loosing only four dead and one medium tank.

All during the day of the 18th Lang attempted to attack, but the German pressure and artillery fire was too heavy. That night he set fire to a house at the edge of town , and the light prevented the Germans from infiltrating in the dark hours. The next morning the Germans attacked with artillery and rockets, but in the face of this Lang managed to advance about 350 yards.

TANK CHIEF BATTERED

That day Lieutenant John F. Gaynor of Ocean Avenue, Freeport, L.I., platoon commander of the 11th Tank Battalion, wore most of the fur off his rabbit's foot. His tank was hit by bazooka fire, setting his machine gun ammunition ablaze, and artillery knocked out his last machine gun.

But under cover of tanks commanded by Sergeant John Shea of 29 Sullivan Place, Bronx, and Sergeant Francis J. Clearly of Roxbury, Mass., Gaynor pulled back and removed machine guns from a knocked out tank to replace his own.

No sooner were the guns in place when another bazooka shell struck his turret.

All that day the Germans attacked and were beaten off. At 4:30 the next morning the Germans massed for a surprise attack. Three times they tried. Three times they were pushed back.

Later that morning the Germans struck northeast and west under heavy artillery fire. For an hour and a half the defenders beat back the Germans, and then just as American ammunition was running low the enemy pulled back to reform.

HALF-TRACKS COME THROUGH

When Lang called back for supplies and ambulances to evacuate his wounded he was told he had been cut off from the rear, but later in the day Sergeant James C. Halligan of Rutherford, N.Y., broke through with two medium tanks and three half-tracks loaded with supplies. With the half-tracks he evacuated the wounded.

And at four that afternoon Lang ordered a withdrawal if possible. He divided his tanks, guns and half-tracks into four units which left at eight-minute intervals under cover of artillery fire, which also covered the noise of his retreat.

He got his entire force out of town without the Germans knowing it, leaving demolitions and mines to delay the enemy further.

HEAVY GUNS GO TO WORK

The Germans didn't discover Berdorf had been evacuated until the next morning, for as soon as Lang had pulled out, the artillery kept pounding it for hours.

By the next morning, however, other American units had dug in on high areas back of the town, further blocking the Germans.

The defense of Berdorf and Echternach, three miles to the southeast, by the 12th Regiment of the 4th Infantry Division stopped the left flank of Von Rundstedt's drive, preventing him from swinging south and grabbing the rich prize of the city of Luxembourg before stronger units could be thrown into line.

············

Reprinted from THE NEW YORK DAILY NEWS, January 5, 1945.
NOTE: It is permissable to send this reprint through the mail.

NOTES FROM THE
ONE HUNDRED THIRD INFANTRY DIVISION

The One Hundred Third Division began its offensive battle from Kircheim on 21 April, 1945, following the advance of the Tenth Armored Division by clearing out bypassed resistance. By 23 April, the One Hundred Third had closed various German escape routes southeast from Stuttgart and reached the Danube River northeast of Ulm on 25 April and crossed it the next day. Also following the Tenth Armored Division was the Four Hundred Eleventh Infantry which took Landsberg, the Four Hundred Ninth reached the Lech River at Lechbruck, and the Four Hundred Ninth cleared Schongau on 28 April. The Tenth Armored Division began negotiations for the surrender of Innsbruck on 2 May as the Four Hundred Ninth Infantry continued forward so as to reach the Inn River at Telf and Zirl the following day.

A LIST OF THE UNITS THAT OUR 10TH ARMORED DIVISION FOUGHT BESIDE OR THROUGH IN THE EUROPEAN THEATER OF WORLD WAR II. (1944 - 1945).

5th Infantry Division
95th Infantry Division
357th Infantry Regiment
6th Armored Division
101st Airbourne Division
609th Tank Destroyer Battalion
769th Armored Anti-Aircraft Battalion
4th Infantry Division
705th Tank Destroyer Battalion
4th Armored Division
94th Infantry Division
456th Infantry Regiment
96th Infantry Division
5th Ranger Battalion
76th Infantry Division
80th Infantry Division
11th Armored Division
12th Armored Division
14th Armored Division
36th Infantry Division
63rd Infantry Division
100th Infantry Division
44th Infantry Division
103rd Infantry Division
65th Infantry Division

268

MAP OF EUROPE

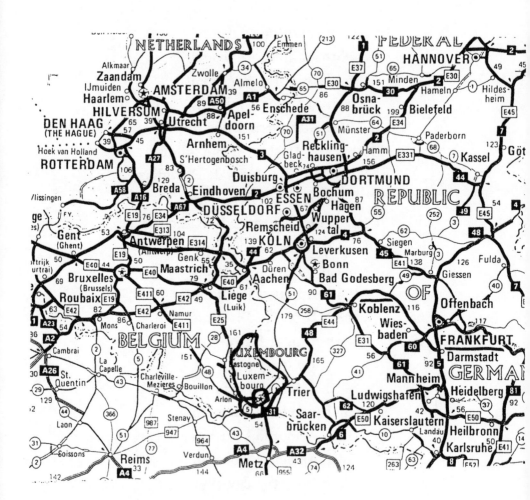

MAP OF LUXEMBOURG

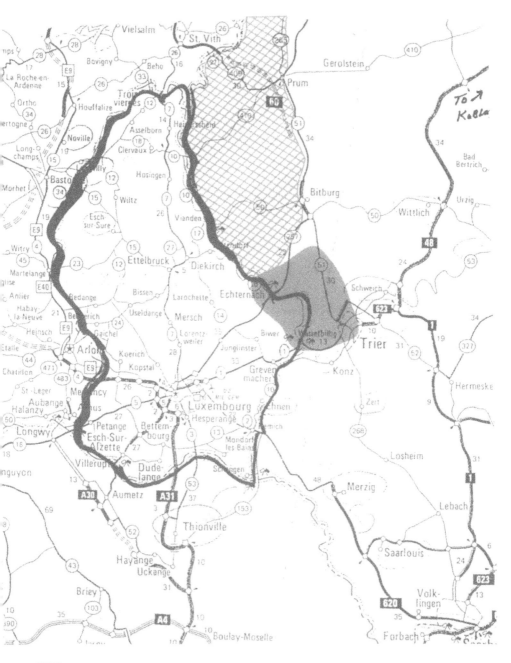

 Approximate location of the
Forest of the Ardennes.

 Approximate location of the "faulted"
structures with their dense evergreen forests.

Fact Sheet
World War II

PROFILE OF U.S. SERVICEMEN
(1941 - 1945)

* 38.8 percent (6,332,000) of U.S. servicemen and women were volunteers.
* 61.2 percent (11,535,000) were draftees. Of the 17,955,000 men examined for induction, 35.8 percent (6,420,000) were rejected as physically or mentally unfit.
* Average duration of service 33 months.
* Overseas Service: 73 percent served overseas, with an average of 16.2 months abroad.
* Combat Survivability (out of 1,000): 8.6 were killed in action, 3 died from other causes, and 17.7 received nonmortal combat wounds.
* Noncombat Jobs: 38.8 percent of the enlisted personnel had rear echelon assignments--administrative, technical, support, or manual labor.
* Average Base Pay: Enlisted: $71.33 per month; Officer: $203.50 per month.

U.S. ACTIVE MILITARY PERSONNEL
(1939 - 1945)
(Enlisted and Officer)

	ARMY	NAVY	MARINES	TOTAL
1939	189,839	125,202	19,432	334,473
1940	269,023	160,997	28,345	458,365
1941	1,462,315	284,427	54,359	1,801,101
1942	3,075,608	640,570	142,613	3,858,791
1943	6,994,472	1,741,750	308,523	9,044,745
1944	7,994,750	2,981,365	475,604	11,451,719
1945	8,267,958	3,380,817	474,680	12,123,455

PEAK STRENGTH OF ARMED FORCES
DURING WORLD WAR II

U.S.	12,364,000	Switzerland	650,000
U.S.S.R.	12,500,000	Rumania	600,000
Germany	10,000,000	Philippines	500,000
(including Austria)		Yugoslavia	500,000
Japan	6,095,000	Netherlands	500,000
France	5,000,000	Sweden	500,000
China		Bulgaria	450,000
Nationalist	3,800,000	Hungary	350,000
Communist	1,200,000	Finland	250,000
Britain	4,683,000	Brazil	200,000
Italy	4,500,000	Czechoslovakia	180,000
India	2,150,000	New Zealand	157,000
Poland	1,000,000	Greece	150,000
Spain	850,000	South Africa	140,000
Turkey	850,000	Thailand	126,500
Belgium	800,000	Iran	120,000
Canada	780,000	Portugal	110,000
Australia	680,000	Argentina	100,000

U.S. ARMED FORCES
TOLL OF WAR
(1939 - 1945)

Killed		Wounded	
Army and Air Force	234,874	Army and Air Force	565,861
Navy	36,950	Navy	37,778
Marines	19,733	Marines	67,207
Coast Guard	574	Coast Guard	432
Total military killed	292,131	Total military wounded	671,278

Merchant Marines			
Died as POWs	37	Dead	5,662
Missing / presumed dead	4,780	Killed at sea	845

ESTIMATED INTERNATIONAL COSTS
OF WORLD WAR II

Battle deaths	14,904,000
Battle wounded	25,218,000
Civilian deaths	38,573,000
Direct economic costs	$ 1,600,000,000,000

COSTS BY INDIVIDUAL NATIONS DIRECTLY
RELATED TO THE WAR (in U.S. Dollars)

U.S.	288,000,000,000	Netherlands	9,624,000,000
Germany	212,336,000,000	Belgium	6,324,000,000
France	111,272,000,000	India	4,804,000,000
U.S.S.R.	93,012,000,000	New Zealand	2,560,000,000
Britain	57,254,226,000	Sweden	2,344,000,000
China	49,072,000,000	South Africa	2,152,000,000
Japan	41,272,000,000	Turkey	1,924,000,000
Italy	21,072,000,000	Switzerland	1,752,000,000
Canada	20,104,000,000	Norway	992,000,000
Australia	10,036,000,000	Portugal	320,000,000

The Supreme Commander talks with men of Company E, 502d Parachute Infantry Regiment, at the 101st Airborne Division's camp at Greenham Common, England, June 5, 1944.

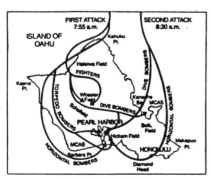

AIRCRAFT PRODUCTION
(All Types)

	1939	1940	1941	1942	1943	1944	1945
U.S.	2,141	6,086	19,433	47,836	85,898	96,318	46,001
Britain	7,940	15,049	20,094	23,672	26,263	26,461	12,070
Soviet Union	10,382	10,565	15,737	25,436	34,900	40,300	20,900
Germany	8,295	10,826	12,401	15,409	24,807	40,593	7,540
Japan	4,467	4,768	5,088	8,861	16,693	28,180	8,263

MILITARY AIRCRAFT LOSSES (1939 - 1945)

U.S.	59,296	France	2,100
Germany	95,000	Canada	2,389
Japan	49,485	New Zealand	684
Britain	33,090	India	527
Australia	7,160	Sweden	272
Italy	4,000	Denmark	154

(U.S.S.R. losses were extremely high, but they were
undisclosed by the Soviet government.)

NAVAL LOSSES (1939 - 1945)
(Submarines, frigates, & all larger ships)
Number of ships

U.S.	157	Germany	672
Britain	296	Japan	433
France	129	Greece	22
Netherlands	40	Yugoslavia	13
Norway	40	*U.S.S.R.	102
Italy	300	Others	36

*Unconfirmed Statistic

MERCHANT SHIP LOSSES
(Ships over 200 tons)

	Numbers
Britain	3,194
Japan	2,346
U.S.	866
Other Allied	1,467
Neutral	902

TANK PRODUCTION
(All Types)

U.S.	60,973
Britain	23,202
Germany	19,926
Italy	4,600
Japan	2,464
U.S.S.R.	54,500

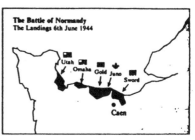

The Battle of Normandy
The Landings 6th June 1944

PRISONERS OF WAR

Prisoners held by the Allies
(excluding those in the Soviet Union):

German	630,000
Italian	430,000
Japanese	11,600

Prisoners held by Germany:

French	765,000
Italian	550,000
British	200,000
Yugoslav	125,000
American	90,000

Prisoners held by Japan:

British	108,000
Dutch	22,000
American	15,000

SOURCES

Robert Goralski, World War II Almanac: 1931 - 1945, G.P. Putnam's Sons, New York, 1981.

Arthur Enock, This War Business, The Bodley Head, London, 1951.

Trade Division, Naval Staff, Admiralty (London), October 1945.

Operations Navy, Division of Naval Intelligence, September, 1945.

50th Anniversary of World War II Commemoration Committee
HQDA, SACC; Pentagon, Room 3E524
Washington, D.C. 20310-0107   (703) 697-4664

BIBLIOGRAPHY

Autobiography	Gen. Omar Bradley
Their Finest Hour	Winston Churchill
A Bridge Too Far	Cornelius Ryan
War as I Knew It	Gen. George Patton
Patton, Ordeal and Triumph	Lodislos Fargo
Impact	Lester Nickles
10th Armored Division Association History	Tom Bubin, Bob Hight, & Lester Nickles
The Ghost Corp Through Hell and High Water	Gen. Walton Walker
Lectures and Tapes	Lt. Gen. Wm. Desobry
My Own Recollections and Notes	Dean M. Chapman
Soldiers of 1944	William McGivern
Master of the Battlefield	Nigel Hamilton
Das Kriegsende	Uwe Jacobi
The 103rd Infantry Division History	Division Personnel
A Horse of a Different Color	Cecil Hill
Some Desperate Glory	Edwin Champion
Blitzkrieg	Len Deighton
Foch Speaks	Charles Bugnet

Printed in the USA
CPSIA information can be obtained
at www.ICGtesting.com
JSHW082227140824
68134JS00016B/769